W9-CRU-876

Living Toward a Vision

LIVING TOWARD A VISION

Hardy R. Denham, Jr.

Broadman Press
Nashville, Tennessee

© Copyright 1980 • Broadman Press.

All rights reserved.

4252-77

ISBN: 0-8054-5277-X

Dewey Decimal Classification: 248.4

Subject heading: CHRISTIAN LIFE

Library of Congress Catalog Card Number: 79-54092

Printed in the United States of America

Dedicated to

HEATHER ELIZABETH

*The tiniest angel in my life
who began the journey of life May 25, 1979*

Unless otherwise noted, all Scripture verses are quoted from the King James Version of the Bible.

Scripture quotations marked RSV are taken from the Revised Standard Version of the Bible, copyrighted 1946, 1952, © 1971, 1973 by the Division of Christian Education of the National Council of the Churches of Christ in the U.S.A., and used by permission.

Scripture quotations marked NIV are taken from the HOLY BIBLE *New International Version*, copyright © 1978, New York Bible Society. Used by permission.

Scripture quotations marked TEV are taken from the *Good News Bible*, the Bible in Today's English Version. Old Testament: Copyright © American Bible Society 1976; New Testament: Copyright © American Bible Society 1966, 1971, 1976. Used by permission.

Contents

1
The Discovery of Life

My son likes to draw mazes, which he gives to me with the challenge that I find the right path from the start to finish. Those of us who have worked this type of puzzle know that it involves a trial-and-error process. A person often makes the wrong turn and finishes at a dead end. Life is like that for many. It is a series of wrong turns and dead ends which leaves the traveler bewildered and confused. The late Bertrand Russell, an agnostic philosopher in Great Britain, said on one occasion, "People are bewildered and don't know how to live a credible life in an incredible world."

Arthur Schopenhauer, the Viennese philosopher, was once sitting on a park bench pondering the profundities of life. Completely wrapped up in the web of his thoughts, he was unaware that a policeman had come up behind him. The policeman tapped him on the shoulder and asked in harsh tones, "Who are you? What are you doing here?" Schopenhauer responded, "I wish I knew." For many, life is a riddle that defies solution.

Men have described life in a variety of ways. Life has been called a nightmare between two nothings and a predicament that precedes death. Christopher Morley said, "Life is a foreign language which all men mispronounce." A scientist wrote that life is a cosmic accident that will someday degenerate back into the void from which it came. A materialist called life a series of possessions that merely fluctuates with time. These statements about life give a clear indication that many people in our world have not discovered it. In traveling the roads of life we often meet people returning from a journey who say to us, "Life is not found there."

Where is life found?

Pleasure

Some people seek life in pleasure. Life for many people is a long weekend of pleasure. One beer commercial declares, "Weekends are made for pleasure." For some, that weekend of pleasure is endless. It must last from Friday until Friday. Solomon sought life in the pursuit and enjoyment of pleasure. He said, "Go to now, I will prove thee with mirth, therefore enjoy pleasure" (Eccl. 2:1). He also said, "Whatever my eyes desired I did not keep from them; I kept my heart from no pleasure" (v. 10, RSV).

Solomon sought meaning for his life in pleasure in two definitive ways. First, he did so by trying liquor. He said, "I searched with my mind how to cheer my body with wine" (v. 3, RSV). Solomon did not become a problem drinker or drink to the degree of becoming an alcoholic. Solomon belonged to the cocktail crowd or the martini mob. He was a member of the gin and tonic team. He sought meaning for life in pleasure as he filled his body with wine.

Another way in which Solomon sought meaning in pleasure was through lust. Sex, which God gave to be the servant of love, became the master of his life. The Bible relates that Solomon had seven hundred wives and three hundred concubines. In case any men are inclined to envy him, remember that seven hundred wives meant seven hundred mothers-in-law. I wonder how Solomon kept up with all the anniversaries and birthdays? But that which God gave to be the servant of love became the master of his life.

Pleasure, or having a good time, has become the religion of America. The golden rule of this new faith is, "If it feels good, do it." The American pleasure bill is astronomical. According to the latest studies, we are now approaching a 10 percent expenditure of our income just for recreation as we serve the religion of pleasure.

But pleasure cannot give meaning to life. Solomon, who lived for the good times, came to say, "Pleasure does you no good" (Eccl. 2:2, TEV). The man who said, "I will cheer my body with wine" came to say, "Wine is a mocker, strong drink is raging: and whosoever is deceived thereby is not wise" (Prov. 20:1). The Bible speaks about the failure of pleasure. It says that the person who is self-indulgent is dead even while he lives (1 Tim. 5:6). The writer of the letter to the Hebrews declared about Moses that he "[chose] rather to share ill-treatment with the people of God than to enjoy the fleeting pleasures of sin" (Heb. 11:25, RSV). The writer did not deny that there are pleasures in sin, but he underscored the fact that these pleasures are not permanent or lasting. They are transitory and fleeting.

The greatest pleasure of all comes from a life relationship with Jesus Christ. The writer of the Psalms declared: "Thou wilt shew me the path of life: in thy presence is fulness of joy; at thy right hand are pleasures for evermore" (Ps. 16:11). Pleasure, instead of being the goal of life, is the product of a good life.

Possessions

There are some who seek meaning for life in possessions. Material possessions are essential for living. In creating us the Lord God gave us a physical nature. This physical nature must be provided for physically and materially. The Lord Christ spoke about man's material needs when he said, "Therefore take no thought, saying, What shall we eat? or, What shall we drink?

or, Wherewithal shall we be clothed? . . . for your heavenly
Father knoweth that ye have need of all these things" (Matt.
6:31-32). The passage deals with the sin of anxiety, but the Lord
Christ acknowledged the need for food, clothing, and shelter.

A great American tragedy is that these and all they represent
have become the goals of life rather than the means of living
life. We have made a mistake in the way we have prioritized
the realities of our existence. During the 1976 presidential cam-
paign, one college student told a reporter: "I'm voting for
_____; he is the candidate who will help me make the
most money." The affluence of our day has led to a material-
mindedness. Beyond question, we have more than any before
us. The median family income in America has increased more
than 300 percent in the quarter of a century from 1950 to 1975,
and the period of largest dollar increase in income has been
since 1965. It is now estimated that there are 240,000 millionaires
in America. That figures out roughly to one millionaire for every
900 Americans.

In the Old Testament there is the report of an interesting
episode during the reign of King Hezekiah. A deputation came
from Babylon to visit Hezekiah, the king of Judah. Hezekiah
showed those men from Babylon the riches of his house. Isaiah,
the prophet, who was something of a court chaplain, asked the
king, "What have they seen in thine house?" Hezekiah responded, "All the things that are in mine house have they seen:
there is nothing among my treasures that I have not shewed
them" (2 Kings 20:15). There is more to be seen in houses today
than ever before. This fact is expressive of the material-minded-
ness of our times.

Alexander Solzhenitsyn, the Russian dissenter, delivered a
commencement address at Harvard University in which he said
that the West had become so obsessed with the material side

of life to the neglect of the spiritual that we had become a weak and hollow people, having little direction or purpose and having lost our capacity for the heroic. These are stinging words by an outsider, but they ring true. Who can deny them? The first question asked by individuals, businesses, governments, and even churches which are faced with decisions is not, "Should it be done?" or "Is it needed?" or "Is it right?" More often the first question is, "How much does it cost?"

Possessions, though essential in life, do not have the power to give life meaning. Solomon, who became one of the richest men in history, declared that the accumulation of wealth was "a striving after wind" (Eccl. 2:11, RSV). What could he have meant by that puzzling statement? Since wind is nothing but air in motion, if one strives after it and succeeds in capturing it, what does he have? Solomon seemed to have been saying, "To base life upon possessions is to base it upon nothing, and to gain possessions is to have nothing." Such a realization was expressed in the suicide note left by a wealthy woman. She wrote, "I have everything to live with but nothing to live for."

The Lord Christ warned about making treasures the goal of life. He said, "Lay not up for yourselves treasures upon earth, where moth and rust doth corrupt and where thieves break through and steal: But lay up for yourselves treasures in heaven, where neither moth nor rust doth corrupt, and where thieves do not break through nor steal: For where your treasure is, there will your heart be also" (Matt. 6:19-21).

A young minister was visiting a middle-aged industrialist who was his friend. The industrialist was showing the young minister through a new factory just completed and put into operation. They walked through the plant amid the whir and whine of machinery. When the tour was completed, the two returned to the office with its luxurious appointments, representative of the industrialist's financial success. The young minister sought to lay the claims of Christ upon the man's heart. The industrialist answered, "This is all the god I'll ever want or need."

A few months later, the young minister walked with the industrialist through the ruins of that same factory. What was left was still smoking from the fire which had consumed it. The owner's impeccable gray business suit was splattered and soiled with water and ashes. The young minister put his arms around him and said, "Bob, your god has gone up in smoke; and mine is still alive." Possessions are important, but they cannot give life. It is possible to have a lot in your purse and absolutely nothing in your person.

A Person

Life is discovered in Jesus Christ. This is what the Lord Christ declared about himself. Jesus said, "I am come that they might have life, and that they might have it more abundantly" (John 10:10). In John 14:6 he said, "I am the way, the truth, and the life: no man cometh unto the Father, but by me." Then he put his finger upon man's failure to have life by saying, "Yet you refuse to come to me that you may have life" (John 5:40, RSV). Where is life found? It is not in pleasure or possessions, but in a person—Jesus Christ.

Life is found only in Christ because he died to provide it and lives to give it. The unknown poet declared the futility of everything but Christ when he said:

> I've tried the broken cisterns, Lord,
> But, ah, the fountains failed;
> And even as I stooped to drink,
> They mocked me as I wailed.
> The frail vessels Thou hast made
> No hands but Thine can fill;

> For the waters of this earth have failed,
> And I am thirsty still.

Solomon, who sought life in the wrong places and practices, came to the realization that life was found only in the Lord. The man who had tried so many things and found them all empty urged others, "Remember now thy Creator in the days of thy youth, while the evil days come not, nor the years draw nigh, when thou shalt say, I have no pleasure in them; While the sun, or the light, or the moon, or the stars, be not darkened, nor the clouds return after the rain: In the day when the keepers of the house shall tremble, and the strong men shall bow themselves, and the grinders cease because they are few, and those that look out of the windows be darkened" (Eccl. 12:1-3). The keepers of the house are the hands. The strong men bent are shoulders stooped with age. The grinders that cease because they are few are the teeth. The windows that become so dim are sight that is almost gone. Solomon was pleading that men remember the Lord and serve him in the freshness of youth, for real life is found in him and in him alone!

The life that Jesus Christ gives is *divine*. The Bible calls it eternal life. The word eternal associated with the Christ life does not speak so much of the quantity of life as it speaks of the quality of life. It is not how long one lives, but the kind of life one has. The Lord Jesus said, "And this is life eternal, that they might know thee the only true God, and Jesus Christ, whom thou hast sent" (John 17:3). The life Christ gives is divine because it is the life of God himself experienced by faith, resulting in the person's becoming the child of God.

The life Jesus Christ gives is *durable*. So much in this world is transitory and passing. So many things do not last. There are things which are here today and then gone forever. But the life in Christ is a lasting life. The Lord Jesus said to his disciples: "My sheep hear my voice, and I know them, and they follow me: And I give unto them eternal life; and they shall never perish, neither shall any man pluck them out of my hand. My Father, which gave them to me, is greater than all; and no man is able to pluck them out of my Father's hand" (John 10:27-29). The apostle Paul wrote of the durability of the life in Christ in his letter to the Roman saints: "For I am persuaded, that neither death, nor life, nor angels, nor principalities, nor powers, nor things present, nor things to come, Nor height, nor depth, nor any other creature, shall be able to separate us from the love of God, which is in Christ Jesus our Lord" (8:38-39). To be sure, the life Christ provides is eternal.

Finally, the life Christ gives is also *dynamic.* It is a life in which there is power and in which one can be productive. Having life in Christ, a person can live to count for something rather than for nothing. Many men and women have expressed the futility of life lived without God.

> So many people come into this world
> Only to be caught in life's mad whirl;
> They live each day at a hectic pace,
> But do little more than occupy space.
>
> When life for them here is done,
> And night ends their frolic and fun,
> The only record about them to abide
> Is that they were born, begat, and died.
>
> When these stand in the Judgment Day
> What a shame that they'll have to say,
> "I was, I was not, nothing more";
> Oh, what a tragedy for life's score.

But the life Christ gives is dynamic. He gives both the summons and strength to become and overcome.

Conclusion

To millions life seems to be a cruel joke. It is a riddle for which no solution seems available. It is a maze of wrong turns and disappointing dead ends. Futilely these millions search for meaning in the pursuit of fleeting and momentary pleasures, the accumulation of possessions, and other such empty exercises. All the while the Lord Jesus stands and says, "I am the life."

There is a book in my study which is difficult to read. I bought it years ago and began reading it. But I put it aside as a boring book and soon forgot it. Then one day I met the author and spent some time talking with him. Later I pulled his book from my shelf and began again to read it. I found the exercise anything but boring. The reason for the change in attitude was the fact that I knew the author of the book. There are a lot of people for whom life is a dull book which they soon lose interest in and put aside. But when you know the author, life becomes thrilling and exciting.

2
The Dedication of Life

Dr. C. Roy Angell told of a wealthy businessman who had an appointment with a certain man. The appointment was for 7:00 P.M. in the man's home. The businessman arrived early and was told that the family was still eating. As he waited he looked at his clothes and wished he had taken the time to shave and clean up. A five-year-old boy came running into the room. Looking the stranger over, he said, "My daddy told me that you are a millionaire. Is that true?" The man answered yes. The boy continued, "He said that you are a self-made man, too. Are you?" Again the man answered yes. Looking the businessman over from his dusty shoes to his unkempt hair, the boy asked, "What did you make yourself like that for?"[1]

The boy asked a question which implies a tremendous truth. We are responsible for our lives. When God gave us life, he also gave the power of self-determination. We decide what we will make of our lives. Many people blame circumstances, situations, or even other people for their having become what they are. However, when one analyzes his situation, he must admit that he is responsible for what he is.

The actor on the stage playing his role held his hands out before himself in a contemplative posture and said, "They're in my hands; all my tomorrows are in my hands." A convicted murderer awaiting execution in the Florida State Penitentiary wrote in a letter, "Man is what he chooses to become. He chooses that for himself." Our lives are in our hands, and what becomes of them is determined by the choices we make.

The Lord Christ recognized man's power to choose. He knew that each person must do something with his life and that the choice was up to the individual. Knowing what should be done in order to experience the best of life, Jesus called men to dedicate themselves to him. "And when he had called the people unto him with his disciples also, he said unto them, Whosoever will come after me, let him deny himself, and take up his cross, and follow me. For whosoever will save his life shall lose it; but whosoever shall lose his life for my sake and the gospel's, the same shall save it. For what shall it profit a man, if he shall gain the whole world, and lose his own soul? Or what shall a man give in exchange for his soul?" (Mark 8:34-37). In calling men to dedication, Jesus Christ said that we can keep life for ourselves and lose it, or we can give our lives to him and find it.

Keep Life and Lose It

The idea in the saving of life which ends in its loss is to keep the life for self and to use it selfishly. The end result of such conduct is the loss of life.

There are so many people who live life with the idea, "My life is mine, and I will do with it what I want; no one must interfere." This is the philosophy expressed in the poem "Invictus."

> Out of the night that covers me,
>   Black as the Pit from pole to pole,
> I thank whatever gods may be
>   For my unconquerable soul.

In the fell clutch of circumstance
    I have not winced nor cried aloud,
Under the bludgeonings of chance
    My head is bloody, but unbowed.

Beyond this place of wrath and tears
    Looms but the horror of the shade,
And yet the menace of the years
    Finds, and shall find me, unafraid.

It matters not how strait the gate,
    How charged with punishments the scroll,
I am the master of my fate:
    I am the captain of my soul.[2]

I knew of a man who voiced the same sentiment. In a situation of choice he went out into his yard, balled up his fist, shook it toward heaven, and shouted, "It's mine, God; it's mine! My life belongs to me, and you keep your hands off it." Perhaps most people who live selfishly, holding onto life for self, are not brash or bold enough to say that to God out loud; but they say it nonetheless by the way they live.

A man went shopping with his wife one day. The shopping trip carried them at last to a five-and-dime store, where nothing can be bought for just a nickel or a dime anymore. The man was tired of following his wife around, so he parked himself by a counter to wait until she was through shopping. It so happened that the counter he stood by was the candy counter. As the man waited, a little boy came into the store and walked up to the counter. The boy was filthy and barefooted. His clothes were old and dirty. It was obvious that he had no money, but he had come into the store to feast his eyes on all the candy behind the glass-encased counter.

The man pulled some money out of his pocket and offered it to the boy. Quick as a flash the boy signaled the salesclerk and spent every cent in the purchase of candy. When the sales-clerk gave the boy the bag of candy, he began to stuff his mouth with as much as it would hold. The man watched the boy for a few seconds and then asked, "Son, may I have a piece of your candy?" The little fellow clutched the bag to his body as if it were the most precious possession in the world and said, "No! It's mine; it's mine!"

That is the way so many people are with their lives. The Lord God himself has given the gift of life and knows the best way for it to be used. When he calls them to dedicate their lives to him, they cry, "No! It's mine; it's mine!"

The Lord Jesus said that to keep life for self is to lose it. The best illustration of this truth in the Bible is the story commonly called the parable of the prodigal son. One day that young man went to his father requesting the share of the family wealth which would be his when the father died. Taking the wealth, the young man went to a far country—he did not want any weekend visitors from home. There he squandered foolishly all he had and ended up in a hog pen. The young man was appropriately labeled "the prodigal"; the word means waster. In selfishly holding on to life, he lost it.

To keep life for self is to lose it because, first, it means keeping life from God. The Lord God made us to live in relationship with him. We were created to become children of God, members of his family.

Ben Hooper once served as the governor of Tennessee. He began life with a strike against him because his mother was not married. The reproach that fell on her fell on him as well. The recesses and lunch periods at school were spent alone because of the taunts of his peers. When he went to town with his mother on Saturday afternoon, people would look at him and ask, "Whose child is he? I wonder who his father is?"

When Hooper was about twelve a new preacher came to town. Everyone was praising the new preacher, and young Hooper went to hear him and was also intrigued. He would go to church late and slip out early because he was afraid the people would say something to him. One Sunday the service was over sooner than he realized, and he was unable to get out ahead of the crowd. Feeling a hand on his shoulder, he turned around and found the preacher looking at him. The minister asked, "Who are you, son? Whose boy are you?" Before Hooper could answer the preacher smiled and said, "Wait a minute. I know who you are. I see the family resemblance. You are a son of God." Then the preacher added with a friendly pat, "Boy, you've got quite an inheritance. Go and claim it."

When a person holds onto his life for himself, he keeps it from God. He loses a family inheritance greater than one can begin to imagine.

Second, when a person keeps life for self, he loses it because he lives by the wrong rules. Everyone must have some rules, standards, or value system by which to live. If he rejects those spelled out in God's Word, he must accept those formulated by men or make up his own. One reason so many people are bewitched, bothered, and bewildered today is that they are making up their own rules for the game of life, and they are changing the rules to suit the times.

John Ehrlichman of Watergate infamy, in an interview with Nick Thimmesch of the *New York Magazine*, said, "I'm more and more realizing that I lived fifty years of my life without ever really coming to grips with the very basic question of what is and what is not right and wrong, what is and what is not valuable and worthwhile."[3] Such is the dilemma of one who keeps life for self.

Third, to keep life for self is to lose it because the life is wasted. Even though years are spent, successes are experienced, and a name is made, it is all for nothing. Guy de Maupassant's story "The Diamond Necklace" tells of a poor but beautiful young wife who borrowed a rich friend's string of diamonds to wear to a ball. The young woman lost the diamond necklace. Her husband borrowed a great sum of money, had the necklace duplicated, and returned it to the owner. The poor couple then worked for years to pay off the great debt. The beautiful young woman was reduced to an ugly, wrinkled, and bent woman. One day, by chance, she met her wealthy friend. They spoke of the diamond necklace, and the woman told her rich friend the truth about the jewels. With a look of pity the rich woman cried, "O, my poor Mathilde. But mine were only paste."

Men lose their lives and live them selfishly to acquire fame and fortunes, but to what end? When they die the fortune is left behind for others to enjoy or waste, and their fame is soon forgotten or eclipsed by another. The life was lost, for it was spent for things which do not last.

Give Life and Find It

The Lord Jesus said, "But whosoever shall lose his life for my sake and the gospel's, the same shall save it." By "losing life" the Lord meant giving it to him. It sounds contradictory to say that one finds something by giving it away, but this is the way it is with life.

The giving of life is not easy. In fact, I believe the Lord's statement that the giving of life to follow him is the most difficult thing he ever told men to do. We speak of this demand so glibly, and many people profess to do this without any realization of all that is involved in the act.

At the close of the morning worship service one Sunday a college student asked for an appointment with me. Because of the note of urgency in his voice I made the appointment for that Sunday afternoon. He came to my office and with virtually no preliminary conversation asked, "What does Jesus Christ want from me?" I told him that the Lord wanted him to give his life in total commitment. It was so easy for me to state this demand of Christ. But how hard it is to carry out! And how much that act of giving self involves.

The Lord made clear his demands in the giving of self. He said, "Whosoever will come after me, let him deny himself, and take up his cross, and follow me." Jesus said that the dedication of life in discipleship demands the denial of self and death to self. To deny self does not mean to withhold from self some desired treasure or experience. Instead, it means to relinquish all rights to your life by turning it over to the Lord. "Self-denial is never just a series of isolated acts of mortification or asceticism. It is not suicide, for there is an element of self-will even in that. To deny oneself is to be aware of Christ and no more of self, to see only him who goes before and no more the road which is too hard for us."[4]

Then Jesus also said that one must die to self. A cross symbolized death in that time, just as an electric chair or hangman's noose does today. This was clearly understood by everyone who heard the Lord say that giving self means to "take up his cross." Josephus, the historian, records that in A.D. 6 a zealot named Judas of Galilee led a band of Jewish nationalists to attack a Roman armory at Stepphoris, just four miles from Nazareth. Roman reaction was swift and brutal. Stepphoris was burned to the ground; the women and children were sold into slavery; and all the men, including Judas and his nationalists, were crucified. Some two thousand men were crucified on crosses which lined the roadways. All of this was in the vicinity of Jesus' hometown, and he was a boy of about eleven or twelve at the time. There is little doubt that he saw those crosses and the men on them. He knew a cross meant death.

When the Lord said, "Take up his cross," he was calling men
to die to self. "When Christ calls a man, He bids him come
and die. It may be a death like that of the first disciples who
had to leave home and work to follow Him, or it may be a
death like Luther's, who had to leave the monastery and go
out into the world. But it is death in Jesus Christ, the death
of the old man at his call."[5]

These two factors in the giving of life—denial of self and
death to self—stress the fact that self-giving is not easy. The
easy thing is to hold onto life, not deny it or die to self. But
this is what Christ demands in his call for dedication.

Let it be understood, however, that Christ does not require
more than he was willing to do. Our giving of self is based on
what he did at Golgotha. The Lord's words about dedication
and the cost of discipleship are prefaced by an announcement
of his own death. "And he began to teach them, that the Son
of man must suffer many things, and be rejected of the elders,
and of the chief priests, and scribes, and be killed, and after
three days rise again" (Mark 8:31). Other statements about his
death supply additional information (Mark 9:31; 10:33-34). Thus
Christ does not demand more of men than he did himself.

The giving of life is hard, but the Scriptures make it clear
that this is the only way to find life. As the Master said, "Whosoever shall lose his life for my sake and the gospel's, the same
shall save it." It is through the giving of self that the life is
saved. God made us creatures of relatedness. That is to say that
we are not capable of living apart from relationships. In order
to survive, a person must rely on resources beyond himself.
This is not debated or doubted in the physical realm of life. It
is even truer in the spiritual realm. A man by himself is only
half a man.

C. S. Lewis told of waking up in the middle of the night

and being unable to go back to sleep. As he lay there he reflected on his condition. It was utterly dark, so there was nothing to see; it was utterly still, so there was nothing to hear; he was utterly alone, so there was no one with whom he could relate. He concluded that nothing could be more threatening to his humanness than such isolation. Then the thought came, "What if I had to live on like this forever and ever?" Such a prospect was more fearful than a thousand burning hells. Lewis said he realized that such an existence was the logical end of leading a totally self-centered life.

In giving life to Christ a person comes into a living relationship with the Lord God. This is what salvation is, and for this reason the Lord said that in giving life one really finds it.

Furthermore, the giving of life results in finding it, for the life dedicated to Christ is the only life worth living. One great tragedy of our times is that for so many people, life is an intolerable burden. People have to put up little placards reminding each other to smile. So many are like the young mother who was seen at a circus with her child. The child was crying, and the mother who was shaking the child could be heard over the noise of the circus saying, "You wanted to come, and you are going to have a good time if it kills you!" It is paradoxical to recognize that more and more time is spent for recreation; yet research studies have revealed that 76 percent of our total leisuretime is spent passively watching others perform. We do not even know how to entertain ourselves.

When life is dedicated to Christ it takes on new meaning. Each day is seen as the day the Lord has made. Because Christ is the center and focus of living, it is a day in which one can rejoice and be glad. Even the inevitable and inescapable problems and difficulties are transformed into opportunities for victory and growth, for Christ is there to help. A beautifully framed parchment which hangs in my office reminds me, "Lord, help me to remember that nothing is going to happen today that You and I together cannot handle."

All our attempts to describe the worthwhile life one experiences when self is dedicated to the Savior fall short. It is truly indescribable. I knew a woman who attended the church where I served. She had made a commitment to Christ in her youth; but, like Jacob, she had strayed. Patiently over a period of several months I sought to lead her back to full commitment. Finally the day came when she gave herself in unreserved dedication. Several weeks later I asked her if she was sorry she had made that decision. "Absolutely not," she answered. "I am thrilled. Living for Jesus is indescribably wonderful. I cannot understand why I waited so long to begin."

Life really begins when you give yourself to Christ. There is a gravestone in a cemetery in Indiana which expresses an unusual message:

> John Evans
> Born 1850, Died 1916
> Age, Two Years

John Evans lived in this world for over sixty years. He gave his life to Christ shortly before he died. Recognizing that that was when life really began for him, he left instructions that his gravestone indicate his age in relation to his discovery of real life.

Conclusion

What can you do with your life? You can keep it for yourself and lose it. Or you can give your life to Christ and find it. But whatever is done with your life is up to you. Your life is in your hands, and the decision is all yours.

Two young men were riding down a highway in an automobile. The highway intersected with a railroad. As they approached the rail crossing, the youth saw that a train was also approaching the crossing. The driver of the car said to his companion, "If I floorboard it, I can beat the train to the crossing and save two minutes." With that he jammed the accelerator to the floor, and the car shot across the tracks just seconds ahead of the oncoming train. The experience unnerved the second boy. When he got his heart out of his throat he asked, "Now, what are you going to do with the two minutes you saved?"

The Lord God has given the gift of life, and the decision of what to do with it is yours to make. Christ calls you to dedicate it to him and thus to save it.

3
The Directions of Life

There once was a farmer in Arkansas who could read and understand the meaning of numbers but not words. Commenting on his handicap, he said, "When I'm going somewhere and pass a road sign, I know how far a town is; but I don't know the name of the town or what direction it's in."

It seems to me that there are a lot of people like this. They are involved in the journey of life and obviously could tell another person something about that journey. They know, for example, when and where they started the journey. They know how long they've been involved in the journey. Furthermore, they can relate some of the experiences they've had in the journey. But the problem is that they don't know where they're going. George Bernard Shaw commented about this type of meaningless existence, "Most men die at thirty, but they are not buried until they are seventy." On a cemetery wall in war-torn Belfast, Northern Ireland, someone wrote the question, "Is there life before death?" For many people the answer is no! There is a meaningless existence before death but not life.

Stop the average person on the street and ask him what his destination and goals in life are. The person will probably answer in terms of what he wants to do that day or where he is going next week. But life? With a shrug of the shoulders and an innocuous "Who knows?" he walks on, meandering from day to day in a mundane and monotonous existence of feeding parking meters, taking coffee breaks, and looking for some exciting new place to spend his next day off. Life before death? Not for that person.

People need a sense of direction to make life meaningful. The person who does not know where he is going can look forward to a long and tiring journey. He will be much like Methuselah (Gen. 5:25-27). In spite of all the years he lived, all that could be said for him was that he was born, begat children, and died. Life for such a person is like a ride on a merry-go-round. Even though time is spent and the going is speedy, the person gets off where he got on.

The Lord God gives direction in life. Having given us the precious gift of life, he did not leave us to our own devices to blunder and stumble through our days. Instead, he spoke words of direction. He did this long ago to a nation who had lost their way and was staggering toward certain destruction. Through his prophet Jeremiah the word was given: "Thus saith the Lord, Stand ye in the ways, and see, and ask for the old paths, where is the good way, and walk therein, and ye shall find rest for your souls" (Jer. 6:16).

There are many directions in which to go. There are many paths from which man can choose. But the directions God gives is to choose "the old paths, where is the good way, and walk therein." The Lord declared that the old paths are still the best.

The direction to walk in the old paths is to be followed. Three pertinent words are in order about this direction.

The Old Paths Are Recommended by God

The person who recommends something to you is important. When someone recommends a product or a plan, you should ask what that person knows about it or if he uses it. We are bombarded by thousands of commercials in which well-known personalities recommend certain products to us. They say, "Use this product; it is better than any other product of its type." I do not know about you, but I really question these commercials and recommendations because I recognize that these well-known personalities are paid fantastic sums of money to say what they do.

A friend of mine went to a doctor for examination. As a result of his examination, the doctor recommended that my friend give up smoking cigarettes. But the doctor had a pack of cigarettes in his shirt pocket as he made the recommendation. Three other doctors had advised him to quit smoking, but all of them had packs of cigarettes showing through their shirt pockets. They all recommended a practice for better health which they did not follow. Needless to say, their recommendations carried very little weight with my friend. The person who recommends something to you is important. When the recommendation is made, one should ask the question, "What does he know about it? Does he do what he recommends?"

The Lord God knew what he was talking about when he said, "The old paths are still the best." A book of instructions is usually packed in the carton or crate with any machine or new appliance. This book of instruction tells the purchaser how to use the product. The instructions also usually include warnings about its misuse. Those instructions say that if you want to get maximum value and benefit out of the product, don't use it a certain way. Such a practice is in order—for after all, who knows more about a product than the individuals who designed and manufactured it?

We have life because the Lord God made us. Some people may choose to regard their lives as a result of some inexplicable accident or an evolutionary process that began with bacteria in garbage left on the earth by unknown space travelers eons ago. Personally, I will stay with the Word of God, which declares: "Then the Lord God formed man of dust from the ground, and breathed into his nostrils the breath of life; and man became a living being" (Gen. 2:7, RSV).

As the psalmist contemplated the majesty of God's creation, he began to wonder about himself. He wrote these words: "When I look at thy heavens, the work of thy fingers, the moon and the stars which thou hast established; what is man that thou art mindful of him, and the son of man that thou dost care for him? Yet thou hast made him little less than God, and dost crown him with glory and honor. Thou hast given him dominion over the works of thy hands; thou has put all things under his feet, all sheep and oxen, and also the beasts of the field, the birds of the air, and the fish of the sea, whatever passes along the paths of the sea" (8:3-8, RSV). When the psalmist considered himself in relation to God's majestic creation, he came to recognize that the Creator God did nothing greater than to make man. The psalmist saw himself as the product of God's creative ability.

Thus, because the Lord God made us and gave us the breath of life, he knows what is best. He recommends the old paths and says that they are still the best.

The Old Paths Lead to the Good Life

The Lord called the old paths "the good way" and said that therein you "shall find rest for your souls." This is not true of all the paths men can walk. The Bible says, "There is a way which seemeth right unto a man, but the end thereof are the ways of death" (Prov. 14:12). However, the directions God gives lead men down the path to a better life.

First, the old paths lead to a *happy life*. Moses blessed ancient

Israel, saying, "Happy are you, O Israel! Who is like you, a people saved by the Lord" (Deut. 33:29, RSV). Some people have the idea that to be a Christian means to have a life that is drab and dull, devoid of happiness.

I saw a television station advertisement on a billboard in Baton Rouge, Louisiana. The advertisement was about comedy programs which could be seen on that channel. The ad pictured a clergyman dressed in black with a reversed collar and a solemn expression on his face. The sign on the ad read, "Our programs can make anyone laugh."

I resent the idea that a Christian does not know how to laugh. The Bible gives a different view of the Christian life than that. The Christian is the only person who can and should be happy. Jesus said, "Now that you know this truth; how happy you will be if you put it into practice!" (John 13:17, TEV).

The old paths God recommends lead to the good life, for Christ defeats the great enemies of happiness. These enemies are worry, boredom, and self-centeredness. So many people are not happy because they are filled with fretful worries, bogged down in boredom, and sour with selfishness. Ralph Barton, the famous cartoonist, left a suicide note which read: "I have run from wife to wife, from house to house, and from country to country in a ridiculous effort to escape myself. . . . I've done it because I am fed up with inventing devices for getting through twenty-four hours every day." Christ sets us free from the killers of happiness.

Second, the old paths lead to a *healthier life*. The Lord God is interested in your health. There is a verse in the Old Testament which a medical doctor used as the topic of a book. "If thou wilt diligently harken to the voice of the Lord thy God, and wilt do that which is right in his sight, and wilt give ear to his commandments, and keep all his statutes, I will put none of these diseases upon thee, which I have brought upon the Egyptians: for I am the Lord that healeth thee" (Ex. 15:26). Dr. S. I. McMillan wrote the book *None of These Diseases* and showed how obedience and faithfulness to God result in a healthier life.

Doctors tell us that there are four things that cut short a person's life. These are obesity, smoking, drinking, and tension. But the result of a life of faithfulness to God is a healthier and longer life. The Bible says, "The fear of the Lord is the beginning of wisdom; and the knowledge of the holy is understanding. For by me thy days shall be multiplied, and the years of thy life shall be increased" (Prov. 9:10-11). The writer of Proverbs also said that keeping God's commandments results in a longer and healthier life (3:1-8).

Dr. George Constock of the Johns Hopkins School of Medicine reported the results of a study in which it was discovered that there is a greater frequency of heart diseases among people who do not go to church or who attend infrequently, as compared to regular church attenders. Walking the path of worship leads to a healthier life.

Third, the old paths lead to a *hopeful life.* Alexander Pope wrote that "Hope springs eternal in the human breast." Man seems to have a natural inclination to hope. If he is sick, he hopes he will get well. If he is poor, he hopes he will strike it rich. If he is lonely, he hopes someone will befriend him.

A number of years ago one of our navy's submarines sank off the Atlantic seacoast. Divers were sent down to assess the damage and to see if any of the crew were still alive. The divers tapped a message on the hull. From within the sunken sub there came a response tapped out in Morse code. The men inside asked, "Is there hope?"

Life proves that hope can be vain and fruitless. Often what we hope for never materializes. Our hope is nothing but a longing for what may or may not come. This is not so when one walks the old path of loyalty to the Lord.

Paul said that the Word of God was written to give us hope (Rom. 15:4). Our salvation in Christ results in our having a lasting hope. Peter wrote, "Blessed be the God and Father of our Lord Jesus Christ, which according to his abundant mercy hath begotten us again unto a lively hope by the resurrection of Jesus Christ from the dead" (1 Pet. 1:3). He said that in Christ we have an ever-living, never-dying hope. Hope in the Bible means a firm and confident persuasion about what will come to be. This is a hope that never fades.

When the Lord God calls us to follow his directions and walk the old paths, he does so for our good. His goal is not to bend and break us in submission but to lead us to the good life.

The Old Paths Must Be Personally Chosen

The decision of which paths you walk in life is largely up to you. This is what the Lord said to the people of ancient Israel. Even though he commanded them to look and ask for the old paths and walk in them, he recognized that whether they did so was really their choice. Whether or not they would do so was up to them personally and individually.

Some of us have walked certain paths in life because we were made to do so. Those who had authority over us made us do certain things. A fellow said to his mother, "I'm not going to school today." She said, "Yes, you are!" He answered, "No! I'm not going to go! All of the students hate me; the teachers criticize me; the superintendent yells at me. I'm not going." His mother responded, "Yes, you are going. You're thirty-three years old; and besides, you're the principal!" Sometimes we have walked paths because others made us do so.

But the choice of which way we go in life is completely up

to us. John Homer Miller said, "Circumstances and situations do color life, but you have been given the mind to choose what the color will be."[1] Whether or not we walk the path of loyalty to the Lord, commitment to his church, behavior based on the Bible, and service for the Savior is up to us.

Where life ultimately ends up is determined by the path chosen. A sign by a heavily traveled dirt road said, "Choose your ruts carefully—you'll be in them for the next ten miles." So the choice of the path determines the destination at which one ultimately arrives.

Dr. Pierce Harris was pastor of the First Methodist Church in Atlanta, Georgia, and one of the greatest Methodist preachers in America. Dr. Harris was once asked to speak at a state penitentiary. He was introduced to the audience of penitentiary inmates by one of the prisoners. In the introduction the prisoner said to his fellow inmates: "I want to tell you a story about two boys. They lived in the same neighborhood; they went to the same school; they played together. They also went to the same Sunday School and church. One of those boys decided he would be smart. He rebelled and quit going to Sunday School and church. He did things he should not have done. The other boy continued on down the path of doing the right things of honoring God and going to Sunday School and church."

The prisoner continued, "Those two boys are now grown men, and both of them are here today. The boy who continued down the right path and remained faithful to the things he had been taught is the great minister who is going to preach to us today. The boy who decided to be smart and rebelled is the prisoner who introduces the preacher to you today."

I am not saying that if one fails to walk the old paths God recommends, he will end up in jail. Nor do I mean to convey that if one walks the good paths, he will end up behind a pulpit.

I am saying, however, that our ultimate destination in life is determined by the paths we choose to walk. Even as one will not ultimately arrive in New York if he sets out toward New Orleans, so you cannot arrive at the destination and goal of life that God has for you if you choose the wrong paths.

Conclusion

While visiting in Washington, D.C., I asked a taxicab driver for directions. He gave me the desired directions in clear terms, and I followed them to the letter. However, I ended up miles from where I wanted to go. That experience emphasized to me that not everyone who gives directions knows what he is talking about.

We need directions for life, and the Lord God gives the right ones. I am told that there is a section in Charlotte, North Carolina, called Myers Park, where the streets turn and twist in a confusing pattern. It is easy to lose one's way in that maze of avenues. However, the section is bisected by a street named Providence Road. Using that road as a point of reference, a person can find his way.

Life presents a complicated and bewildering choice of paths to walk. Many of these end at the precipice of ruin. However, in the midst of that bewildering maze of paths, there is one marked Providence Road. If one walks that road he discovers the good life. The Bible calls men to the old paths recommended by the Lord in which he gives the needed direction. "Trust in the Lord with all thine heart; and lean not unto thine own understanding. In all thy ways acknowledge him, and he shall direct thy paths" (Prov. 3:5-6).

4
The Development of Life

A pastor was once asked to speak to the children of his church on the subject of what the Bible says about life in this world—this journey we are all making from the womb to the tomb. He made two affirmations to the children. "According to the Bible, life gets better and better as it goes along. At the same time, the Bible says that life gets harder and harder as it progresses." These two statements declare that life is not a static experience or one that stays the same. Instead, life is a constantly changing experience.

Life for the Christian is to be a continuous process of becoming. The experience of salvation, or new birth, is just the beginning of this journey. So many people look on salvation as a goal. Once they have experienced it, they think they have reached the goal. The biblical view of salvation is that it is a beginning, not an end. Having new life in Christ, the Christian is to grow daily to become more and more like the Master.

The Bible emphasizes that the Christian life is a becoming process. When the Lord Jesus called Simon Peter and Andrew to follow him, he said, "Come ye after Me, and I will make you to become fishers of men" (Mark 1:17). Notice that following Jesus did not automatically make them fishers of men. Instead, this is what they would become as the result of a developed life. In an autobiographical passage Paul wrote to the Philippians about his own pilgrimage in faith. About his desire to become like Christ he said, "Not that I have already obtained all this, or have already been made perfect, but I press on to take hold of that for which Christ Jesus took hold of me. Brothers, I do not consider myself yet to have taken hold of it. But one thing I do: Forgetting what is behind and straining toward what is ahead, I press on toward the goal to win the prize for which God has called me heavenward in Christ Jesus" (Phil. 3:12-14, NIV). The great apostle affirmed that he was a becomer.

The letter to the Hebrews was written to people who had stopped in the becoming process. The key verse in the letter reads, "Therefore let us leave the elementary doctrines of Christ and go on to maturity" (Heb. 6:1, RSV). This verse identifies a problem and sounds a challenge. The problem was arrested development. The Hebrew Christians had stopped short of becoming all they had the potential to become in Christ. The late Harry Stack Sullivan, pioneer psychiatrist, said, "Most people are caricatures of the persons they might have been." This was true of those first-century saints. The challenge given by the writer of the letter was for the believer to go on in the process of development. He challenged them to go on becoming.

How can a person become all he has the potential to become? To be sure, no person ever fully maximizes his potential. Erich Fromm wrote, "It is part of the tragedy of the human situation that the development of self is never completed; even under the best conditions only part of man's potentialities is realized. Man always dies before he is fully born." [1] However, it is possible for us to become more than we are and to strive to become what we should be. The writer of Hebrews gave insight into how this challenge to become can be met. He wrote, "Wherefore, seeing we also are compassed about with so great a cloud of witnesses, let us lay aside every weight, and the sin which doth so easily beset us, and let us run with patience the race that is set before us, Looking unto Jesus the author and finisher of our faith; who for the joy that was set before him endured the cross, despising the shame, and is set down at the right hand of the throne of God" (Heb. 12:1-2).

There are four imperatives for the development of life. These are to choose right goals, discard excess weight, refuse to quit, and look to Christ.

Choose Right Goals

Life is often compared to a journey—a journey from the womb to the tomb. This is a valid comparison. Like a journey, a life is to have goals toward which one moves. Who would begin a journey without having a destination in mind? Credible living means having goals toward which one reaches.

Having goals for life is not only sensible; it is essential. It is equally imperative that a person select the right goals. It has been said that we usually get what we strive for; and in the process of striving, we are making of ourselves what we ultimately become. Your life today is what the experiences of yesterday have made it, even as your tomorrow is being largely determined by how you live today. Thus, having the right kind of goals is important.

There are three truths about goals worth attention. First, goals give us a reason for living. A goal is a star in the eyes which puts fire in the heels. Goals motivate to action; they give a sense of purpose to living.

Second, goals keep the life on course. The person who knows where he is going is less likely to be detoured in the journey of life. During pioneer days a westward-bound wagon train came to a river which had to be crossed. The river was wide, though not very deep, and the water was very swift. One by one the wagon masters urged the oxen pulling the wagons into the river. Because of the swift flow of the current, however, the teams and wagons emerged from the river far downstream.

One wagon master saw what was happening. He stopped his team at the edge of the river and looked across to the distant bank. The man chose a tree on the far side of the river and, with his sight focused on that goal, he urged his team into the river. The flow of the current pushed against his team and wagon as it had the others; but he kept his eyes on the tree on the distant bank, guiding the oxen toward it. As a result he and his wagon came out of the river on the trail, not hundreds of yards downstream.

The contrary flow of life can be strong at times. There are situations and pressures which can cause men to wander from the course. But when a person has a goal toward which he is daily moving, he is less likely to get off course.

Third, goals must be worthy. Life is destroyed rather than developed if one foolishly chooses the wrong goals. Esau, the firstborn son of Isaac, was a perfect example of a man who had the wrong goals. He was a man who would appeal to many people today—rugged, rough, and ready for the daring deed. But the vast potential of his life was prostituted and wasted because his goals were so wrong. A good time and a full stomach were all that mattered to him. The wrong goals can lead to the shipwreck of life.

The goal of the Christian's life is to become like Christ. All of us have our individual goals in terms of our purposes. However, becoming more like the Master is to be the overriding goal in life for every believer. This is what Paul was saying about himself to the Philippian saints. This is also what the Lord God saved us to become.

Many Christians identify Romans 8:28 as their favorite Scrip-

ture verse. It expresses a great message about God's ability to
work in all situations of life for the believer's good. But to what
end does the Lord God work? The next verse, Romans 8:29,
tells this: "For whom he did foreknow, he also did predestinate
to be conformed to the image of his Son." Paul wrote that God's
working for our good in all things is to the goal that we become
more like Jesus. Since this is a goal for which we were saved,
and the goal of God's working in our behalf, this must also be
the goal of our living.

Discard Excess Weight

The author of Hebrews looked on life as a race in which
one runs. Perhaps he was familiar with the races that were part
of the Greek athletic contests. The analogy of life's being like
a race is a good one. Runners in a race do not carry excess
weight. They wear a minimum of clothing and carry nothing
on their backs or in their hands. The same care must be taken
if one is to daily maximize his potential in life.

Norman Vincent Peale wrote that modern-day Romans have
an unusual New Year's practice. On New Year's eve they throw
out of their houses everything that is no longer usable. Broken
articles and worn-out utensils are all thrown away. The idea
in the practice is to not enter the new year encumbered with
the trash of the old. The process of developing life demands
the same practice. If one is to become all he has the potential
to become, he must discard excess weight.

First, the sins of life must be discarded. The writer of Hebrews
urged people to "throw off everything that hinders and the sin
that so easily entangles" (12:1, NIV). When the Lord Jesus called
blind Bartimaeus to come to him, Bartimaeus threw off his garment (Mark 10:50). He got rid of a garment which would have
gotten in his way in his attempt to get to Christ. Sins in the

life do just that. These must be discarded.

One part of discarding our sins is to put them behind us once they have been forgiven. The Lord God is far more gracious to men than some are to themselves. When God forgives, he forgets. It is one thing for a Christian to be forgiven and another to accept the fact that he is forgiven. There are people who daily indict themselves for sins which they have already confessed and which God has forgiven. Failing to close the book on sins God has forgiven is to carry excess baggage which weighs a person down.

Second, past accomplishments must also be put aside. The person who continues to relive some achievement in the past will not do much about making new records in the present. All of us have known people who talk of little more than some past moment of glory. They are like the college star quarterback who fifteen or twenty years later is still running the play that won the championship game.

While attending a meeting of state education commission chairmen, I met a Baptist layman who had served as chairman for one of our state conventions. This man had retired from his profession and devoted his retirement years to Christian education in his state. He told a group of us that when he retired he took all the plaques, awards, and recognitions given him in his professional career and boxed them. He stated that he did not want to spend his retirement years preoccupied with the memories and reminders of the past.

The experiences learned in the yesterdays of life are valuable and will serve us well as we face the challenges of today and tomorrow. But if one holds onto the accomplishments of yesterday, he will not do much about the possibilities in today.

Third, resentment and hurt feelings over injustices done must be discarded. Every person must learn to deal with negative feelings. None of us is immune to the possibility of resentment. But a grudge is a heavy load to carry and does the bearer much more harm than the one against whom it is held. King Saul never became the leader he had the potential to be. It is possible to identify several reasons, not the least of which is the fact that he wasted so much of his time and energy trying to eliminate David. Saul resented David because of his popularity, and that resentment cost the king dearly. Negative attitudes are like weights on the soul that must be cast off.

I read about a man who planned the perfect murder. He killed his victim in one place. Making sure he left no traces, he put the body in the trunk of his car and drove several hundred miles to a deserted beach. He put the body on his shoulders and waded out into the ocean until the water was up to his chin. Then he tried to throw the corpse off into the water, but he discovered that he could not. Rigor mortis had set in, and the murderer could not free himself of the body. The dead weight of the victim pulled him down, and he drowned. There are weights which have the same effect on life. If these are not discarded, one is stunted in the development of his life.

Refuse to Quit

The writer urged the Hebrew saints to "Run with patience the race that is set before us" (12:1). The word translated patience means endurance or perseverance. The meaning is that the believer is not to be a quitter in the race of life. This is what some of them had done. The writer issued the challenge to go on and keep on going.

Men who become something in life have this characteristic in common—they refuse to quit. When Herbert Hoover was being presented the Horatio Alger Award he was asked, "Mr. President, can you state in one sentence the secret of your success in life?" He answered, "With the help of God, I never gave up."

When Captain Eddie Rickenbacker was being presented the same award, he was asked the secret of his success. He replied, "My mother, a very poor woman in Columbus, Ohio, taught her kids to pray, to read the Bible, to follow Jesus Christ, and never to give up."

Once Rickenbacker was in a place crash in Atlanta. He was taken to a hospital, where he was pronounced in critical condition. Everyone thought he would die. Walter Winchell, the famous radio commentator, said in a broadcast, "Friends, pray for Eddie Rickenbacker. He is dying in an Atlanta hospital. He is not expected to live out the night." Rickenbacker was listening to the broadcast. It is reported that he threw a water pitcher at the radio and said, "I'm not going to die. I'm not going to give up."

Admiral Richard E. Byrd was one of America's great explorers. He was also a man who did not know the meaning of the word quit. From his youth Byrd had the ambition to be an explorer. But while in college he broke a foot and crushed his ankle. He overcame those injuries and was able to win a commission in the United States Navy. However, when his old lameness reappeared, he was retired from the service at the age of twenty-eight as physically unfit. Byrd decided that he would force his way back in active service by becoming a pilot. Soon he was back on active duty as a flyer and a specialist in lighter-than-air craft. But again his ambitions were thwarted, for he was retired from the navy a second time because of the same bad foot. Richard Byrd then obtained private capital to finance expeditions. In spite of his obstacles, he flew across the Atlantic and planted American flags at both the North and South Poles. Finally the service from which he was twice retired bestowed on him the rank of admiral. He had refused to quit.

Rocky Bleier of the Pittsburg Steelers is well known to football fans. He is not the run-of-the-mill professional football player. Bleier served in the army in Vietnam. While on patrol he was hit in the left thigh by small-arms fire. Then a grenade exploded at his feet. Shrapnel tore into both legs, shattering bones in his right foot. Even though he was not permanently crippled, army doctors told him he would never run again. Bleier had the goal of playing running back for the Steelers. It took weeks of agonizing discipline before he could run any distance, and two years of hard work before he was able to earn his position on the championship team. But he did it because he refused to quit.

There are times when we all would like to quit. It may be because of disappointment or failure or just getting tired. But the winners in life are those who would not quit. When Archie Moore was asked what it took to become a championship boxer, he answered, "Fight one more round." Someone wrote:

> When things go wrong as they sometimes will,
> When the road you're trudging seems all uphill,
> When the funds are low and the debts are high,
> And you want to smile, but you have to sigh,
> When care is pressing you down a bit,
> Rest if you must, but don't you quit.
> Life is queer with its twists and turns,
> As every one of us sometimes learns,
> And many a failure turns about
> When he might have won had he stuck it out;
> Don't give up though the pace seems slow—
> You may succeed with another blow.
> Success is failure turned inside out—
> The silver tint of the clouds of doubt,
> And you never can tell just how close you are,
> It may be near when it seems so far;

So stick to the fight when you're hardest hit—
It's when things seem worst that you must not quit.

Look to Christ

The goal of the Christian's life is to be like Jesus Christ. But we cannot become more like Christ unless we look to him. The Hebrew Christians were urged to keep "Looking unto Jesus the author and finisher of our faith" (12:2). The act of looking means more than having him as our goal. It also means depending on him to achieve that goal.

There is a profound truth in this admonition. A person cannot look to Christ and at the same time pay heed to the obstacles which hinder. Matthew reported that when Jesus walked on the water to his disciples in the boat, Peter said, "Lord, if it be thou, bid me come to thee on the water" (Matt. 14:28). The Lord told Peter to come, and the disciple actually got out of the boat and started walking on the water toward Jesus. However, when Peter became aware of the wind and water around him, he became afraid and began to sink. Part of Peter's problem was that he took his eyes off the Lord and stopped depending on him.

So many times we fail in the work of becoming because we do not rely on the Lord. When the Lord Jesus and three of his disciples were on the mount of transfiguration, the other nine disciples waited at the foot of the mountain. A father came bringing his afflicted son. Since the Lord was not there, he asked the remaining disciples to heal his son. They failed in their attempt and in so doing were humiliated before the people. When Jesus and the three descended, he did what his disciples could not do—he healed the boy. Later the nine disciples asked Jesus why they had failed in their attempt to heal the afflicted son. He answered, "This kind can come out only by prayer" (Mark

9:29, NIV). Jesus said their failure in service was due to their failure to depend upon God. They attempted to do in their own strength something which could only be done with God's help.

Since our goal in the development of life is to become more like Christ, it is important that we look to him. In so doing we become like him. There is an ancient legend about a hump-backed king whose affliction had caused him to become a bitter man. His ill temper led him to do things which made his subjects unhappy. The king could think of little but his bent, misshapen body as he walked the gardens and corridors of his palace, planning more oppressive laws out of sheer malice.

One day a sculptor came and asked permission to carve an image of the king's head. The king ordered, "Carve a statue of me from head to foot but without my curse—make me as I might have been." The sculptor carved the statue in pure white marble and made the figure regal and perfect in stature. The statue was put in a secret place in the garden by a pool.

Every day the king went to the secret place and stood for hours, contemplating the statue of his ideal self. As the time passed and the king continued this daily contemplation of his ideal self, the people began to wonder, "What has come over our ruler? He is kind and gracious, not harsh and mean." Then they began to whisper, "What has happened to his back? He doesn't look deformed anymore." The king heard their whispers and raced to the pool. He looked at his image in the water and saw that he was no longer deformed. Instead, he stood straight and erect, just like the statue of his ideal self.

The Lord Jesus is our goal and guide in the process of becoming. Success demands that we depend on Christ, looking to him as we daily meet him in our own secret places.

Conclusion

The journey from the womb to the tomb is one in which life becomes better and harder. This is because the pilgrimage of life is a daily process of development—one in which we are to be becomers. The ringing challenge of the Scriptures is that each of us will go on in the process of development. We are to do so with the realization that becoming is an activity which is never finished, but one in which each day should find us farther along than the day before.

This challenge of the development of life can be met if we have the right goals, discard excess weight, refuse to quit, and look to Christ. These are mandates for becomers.

5
The Devotions of Life

When the Hell Gate Bridge spanning the East River in New York was being built, the engineers discovered that there was an old, forgotten, sunken, wrecked ship embedded in the mud of the river bottom. The wreck was right at the point where one of the strategic bridge piers was to be placed. The wreck had to be removed, so powerful tugboats were secured and chains were attached to it. The tugboats, whose engines produced thousands of horsepower, could not budge the sunken vessel.

Then one of the engineers had an idea. A large flatboat which had been used to float some of the building materials to the construction site was brought over the wreck at low tide. Chains from the flatboat were lowered to be attached to the wreck embedded in the mud of the river bottom. Then the engineers backed off to wait for the tide to come in.

What the machines of men could not accomplish, the irresistible force of the tide did accomplish. As the tide flowed in, it lifted that flatboat, which in turn pulled the wreck loose from the mud of the river bottom. The vessel was then floated out to sea and released to sink.[1]

Love is an irresistible force that motivates men to do what no other force in this world can cause them to do. It was love of freedom that motivated Patrick Henry to say in the Virginia House of Burgesses, "Give me liberty, or give me death." It was love for this country that led Nathan Hale, the schoolteacher turned Revolutionary War spy, to say before being executed by the British, "I only regret that I have but one life to lose for my country." It was love for men that led Jesus Christ to the cross.

To live in the Lord is to live in love. But the love about which the Bible speaks is not a sweet sentimental spirit, a tug at the heart, or a lump in the throat. Instead, biblical love is active. It is not something one feels, but what a person does.

The Bible teaches that there are three focuses of love. This is seen in the answer the Lord Jesus gave a lawyer. The man asked a question about Commandments. Jesus answered, "Thou shalt love the Lord thy God with all thy heart, and with all thy soul, and with all thy mind. This is the first and great commandment. And the second is like unto it, Thou shalt love thy neighbour as thyself" (Matt. 22:37-39). The Christian is commanded to love himself, love God, and love others.

Love Yourself

The command to love self seems incompatible with the fact that we are to deny self and turn from selfishness. This is not true. Erich Fromm wrote that "Selfishness and self-love, far from being identical, are actually opposites." [2]

Love for self is nonexistent in the lives of many people. Cecil Osborne wrote that most people dislike themselves, whether they know it or not.[3] A woman went to see her pastor about a problem she had. She found fault with everything. The pastor responded to the statement of her problem by asking, "Why do you hate yourself?" The woman was shocked and denied that she did hate herself. But the more she thought about it, the more she came to see that her negative feelings about everything came about because she did hate herself.

Loving self is basic in the matter of loving. A person cannot love God or others unless he first loves himself. Dr. Smiley Blanton defined love as a positive interest in something. You cannot have a positive interest in someone if you have a negative attitude about yourself. To love means to give yourself. You cannot give yourself if you do not feel you are a person worth giving.

The Lord Jesus accepted self-love as a fact of life and a fact that is acceptable. He said, "Love your neighbor *as yourself.*" Another way of stating that text is, "Love your neighbor as you love yourself" (TEV). Jesus did not say, "You love yourself; love your neighbor instead." He said, "You love yourself; love your neighbor as well."

People need to learn to love themselves. There are three vital essentials for self-love. First, you must *accept yourself.* This means coming to terms with yourself or accepting the you that you are.

Many people are busy rejecting themselves. Dr. Wayne W. Dyer in his book *Your Erroneous Zones* identified some behavior patterns which spell self-rejection. Refusing to accept a compliment, giving credit you are due to another, and needing your opinions supported by another are expressions of self-rejection.

You can never love yourself as Jesus taught until you first accept yourself. You can accept yourself when you realize that God does. God loves you! The Lord God does not love you for the reasons we love each other. God loves you because you are you. When a person realizes that God accepts him as he is, then he can begin to accept himself.

Second, in order to love yourself you must *believe in yourself.* You must believe in yourself as a person of infinite value. Frank Pollard quoted the man who said, "I'm somebody, 'cause God don't make no junk." How much is a person worth? Jesus asked,

"For what shall it profit a man, if he shall gain the world, and lose his own soul? Or what shall a man give in exchange for his soul?" (Mark 8:36-37). The Lord said that you are worth more than the world and its combined wealth.

If you are to love yourself, you must also believe in yourself as a person who is better than you sometimes think. All of us are sinners, yet sometimes we are too hard on ourselves. We can think we are no good, totally wicked, and beyond hope. That isn't true! The truth of the matter is that we are a strange mixture of good and bad, right and wrong. The prodigal son was bad enough to reject his father, but good enough to come to his senses and beg forgiveness.

Third, to love yourself you must *conduct yourself*. Self-love is related to behavior. When one doesn't live as he thinks he should, he doesn't like himself. Cecil Osborne wrote that one step to loving yourself is to "do the things that will make you like yourself better." [4]

Love God

To love the Lord God is the primary commandment in the Scriptures. The lawyer who questioned Christ sought to involve him in a rabbinical dispute over laws. The scribes had gone through their Scriptures with a fine-toothed comb, seeking to count all the laws in the Old Testament. They had identified a total of 613 laws, 365 of which were negatives—"Thou shalt not." There was a "Thou shalt not" for every day in the year. Almost 250 of the 613 laws were positives—"Thou shalt."

Having identified all these laws in the Scriptures, the scribes then attempted to rank them in the order of their importance or priority. They disagreed over the order and spent hours in debate over the issue of which law should be first. The lawyer's question was designed to involve Jesus in this dispute. Thus he asked, "Master, which is the great commandment in the law?" (Matt. 22:36).

The Lord's answer identified love for God as the greatest of all commandments. He said, "Thou shalt love the Lord thy God with all thy heart, and with all thy soul, and with all thy mind" (v. 37). Jesus quoted Deuteronomy 6:5, a significant passage to the Jews. He stated that what was true in the past is always true—men are to love God with their whole being.

Our love for God is a responsive love. Loving the Lord is not something man automatically does. We do not come into this world with an inclination toward loving God. Instead, we come to love the Lord because he first loved us.

The Bible teaches that God is love (1 John 4:8). We love because the God of love makes us able to do so. Thus our love for God is a responsive love. John wrote, "Herein is love, not that we loved God, but that he loved us, and sent his Son to be the propitiation for our sins" (1 John 4:10).

If the Lord God had not made the first move toward us because of his love for us, we would never be able to love him. Paul wrote of his own experience in which the love of Christ constrained him (2 Cor. 5:14). God's love reached out and took control.

It is in God's love that we come to understand the true meaning of love. It is because of God's love that we are able to love ourselves, the Lord, and other people.

The love we are commanded to have for God is expressed by obedience. The Lord spoke through Moses and said, "I command thee this day to love the Lord thy God, to walk in his ways, and to keep his commandments and his statutes and his judgments, that thou mayest live and multiply" (Deut. 30:16). Love for God would be expressed by walking in his ways and obedience to his commands.

The Lord Jesus told his disciples, "If ye love me, keep my commandments" (John 14:15). He added, "If a man loves me, he will keep my word," and "He who does not love me does not keep my words" (John 14:23-24, RSV). The Lord was saying that our love for him will be expressed by our obedience to him. Our love for God is not measured by how beautifully we sing the songs of love in church but by how we behave. It is not how we talk in church but how we walk in the world that offers conclusive evidence of our love for the Lord.

Love People

When questioned by the scribe, the Lord also identified the second greatest commandment. "And the second is like unto it, Thou shalt love thy neighbour as thyself" (Matt. 22:39). Paul wrote, "Owe no man any thing, but to love one another: for he that loveth another hath fulfilled the law" (Rom. 13:8).

Jesus impressed on his disciples their responsibility to love each other. "A new commandment I give unto you, That ye love one another; as I have loved you; that ye also love one another. By this shall all men know that ye are my disciples, if ye have love one to another" (John 13:34-35).

What did the Lord Christ mean when he said, "A new commandment"? The command to love others is as old as Leviticus 19:18. Jesus did not mean that the commandment is new in time but in kind. The new aspect in the commandment is the standard for loving others. The disciples were told, "You love one another; even as I have loved you, that you also love one another" (John 13:34, RSV).

The Lord's love for his disciples was *a faithful love*. The lack of perfection in man demands forgiveness. The very night Christ spoke this commandment to love, Simon Peter denied him. After our Lord rose from the tomb on Sunday morning, an angel met the women who had come to finish burial preparations, and told them, "Go . . . , tell his disciples and Peter" (Mark 16:7). Peter was a disciple—he was one of the group. But the angel specified Peter as if to emphasize that he was loved and forgiven.

Christian love is forgiving love. Forgiveness is difficult, even for a Christian. When a person refuses to forgive someone who has wronged or hurt him, he is saying by that refusal, "I think more of myself and the injury done me than I do you." But love is putting the needs of others before self. In the situation of injured and ruptured relationships, this means forgiving.

Christ's love was faithful in its endurance to the end. The chapter in which the text is recorded begins with the statement, "Now before the feast of the passover, when Jesus knew that his hour was come that he should depart out of this world unto the Father, having loved his own which were in the world, he loved them unto the end" (John 13:1). The statement "He loved them to the end" speaks volumes about love.

One of the saddest facts about life is that love can die. As a pastor, far too many times I have been called to minister at the funeral of love for a couple who failed to nurture and care for their love. More than a million times a year in America a judge's gavel falls; and with two words, "Divorce granted," the announcement is made that love can die. But not God's love. The Lord said through the prophet Jeremiah, "I have loved thee with an everlasting love" (Jer. 31:3). Christ was faithful in his love for those men, for he loved them to the end.

Then the Lord's love for his disciples was *a forgetful love*. The Lord Jesus had just washed the disciples' feet (John 13:4-5). When a guest arrived at a house, his feet would be hot and dirty because of the type of sandals worn. It was an act of hospitality for the host to provide for the washing of his guests' feet. Thus the washing of the disciples' feet was not unusual. The unusual thing was that Jesus did it.

Christ was the host at that Passover supper. The washing of feet was ordinarily done by a servant, not by the host. But Jesus the host became Jesus the servant. He forgot who he was. He forgot the fact that he was the Lord, and in so doing he taught his disciples that Christian love is self-forgetting.

This is a difficult thing for us because we are caught up with and in ourselves. But as the Lord Jesus emphasized to his disciples this commandment that they love one another, he stressed the ideal of self-forgetting love—the willingness to forget self in behalf of another.

Most of us know John 3:16. But do we know 1 John 3:16: "By this we know love, that he laid down his life for us; and we ought to lay down our lives for the brethren" (RSV)? Christ taught this kind of self-forgetting love for people.

Conclusion

The tide was an irresistible force that lifted the sunken vessel from the mud so that the bridge could be built. Love is a powerful force which motivates us to do what law cannot make us do or what government cannot force us to do. No wonder Paul said, "So faith, hope, love abide, these three; but the greatest of these is love" (1 Cor. 13:13, RSV).

6
The Decisions of Life

Life is filled with stress situations. In learning to live, a person must learn how to deal with stress. Stress can be a tool that can help build a credible life or a weapon that can destroy life. The necessity of making a decision is one of the most common stress situations in life. The greater the decision and its consequences, the greater the degree of stress associated with it. This was recognized by the Quaker theologian Elton Trueblood in a talk he gave called "The Agony of Choice." Robert Browning in *The Ring and the Book* has a character say, "Life's business is just the terrible choice."

Gideon found himself in a stress-producing situation of decision. Gideon lived in that period in Jewish history after Joshua had led the people of Israel into the land of Canaan, but prior to the time of Samuel when the kingdom was established and a monarchy was set up. It was that time about which the writer of the Judges wrote, "In those days there was no king in Israel; every man did what was right in his own eyes" (Judg. 17:6, RSV). It was a turbulent, unstable, confused period in Jewish history, and the people were repeatedly oppressed by different alien nations.

In Gideon's time the oppressors were the Midianites. One day, as Gideon was busy about the everyday business of life, the angel of the Lord appeared to him. This angel of the Lord is identified in the narrative as none other than the Lord himself. The angel was a theophany, a preincarnation appearance of the Lord Christ. The angel announced to Gideon the Lord's intention to do something about Israel's plight and stated that it was God's intent to use Gideon as a human instrument in doing something to alleviate that situation of oppression. Thus it was that Gideon was confronted with the command and commission of God that he become an instrument in the deliverance of God's people. Would Gideon decide to accept the assignment, or would he decide to refuse it? That day in the winepress where he worked, he found himself in the stress situation of making a decision.

In this episode in Gideon's life we can discover some vital principles to be applied when we must decide. Notice that a decision is to be governed by faith and not fear; a decision is to be governed by reason and not reaction; and a decision is to be governed by providence and not propaganda.

When you must decide, make sure your decision is:

Governed by Faith, Not Fear

Gideon was afraid because of the enormity of the assignment. Gideon wanted a sign, even though it was the Lord God who spoke to him. He was afraid to act on what the angel of the Lord said and asked God for proof that the Lord indeed was summoning and commissioning him to act redemptively in the midst of that turbulent situation. Gideon sought proof by which his fears could be calmed.

Before he would undertake the assignment, he put God to the test. He laid out the fleece one night and said to the Lord, "If thou wilt save Israel by mine hand, as thou hast said, Behold, I wilt put a fleece of wool in the floor; and if the dew be on the fleece only, and it be dry upon all the earth beside, then shall I know that thou wilt save Israel by mine hand, as thou hast said" (Judg. 6:36-37). The next morning when Gideon arose and went out to the threshing floor, he discovered that the fleece was saturated with dew but that the ground surrounding it was dry.

But still he was afraid to undertake the assignment. He said to the Lord a second time, "I pray thee . . . let it now be dry only upon the fleece, and upon all the ground let there be dew" (v. 39). And it was so. Those tests underscore the depth of Gideon's fear in the face of God's call.

Every person has experienced fear. We often think that some people are not afraid. There are some folks who give the illusion that they live without fear. They put on a happy face. They adopt a carefree attitude about life. They appear to be so courageously bold in the things they do. This causes us to think that they are not afraid. But if you look beyond the facade of the happy face, underneath that carefree attitude, and delve into the depths of that apparent bold and courageous conduct, you will find a person who is afraid.

Fear is a common experience, for every man knows fear by its first name. Fears are not all bad, and in some situations they can help us in the stress-producing decision. Fear can keep one from being rash in behavior. The fear of falling keeps me off the roof. Fear can serve a person well in the living of his days, yet fear is not to rule in the time of decision. If Gideon had taken the counsel of his fears and no other counsel, he would not have done what the Lord told him to do. He would never have become God's deliverer for his people in the face of the oppression of the Midianites.

When men decide on the basis of fear, they usually decide wrongly. The Lord Jesus told a story we call the parable of the talents. It is found in Matthew 25:14-30. In the story Jesus told about a very wealthy man who was going to take a leave of absence. He called in three of his trusted servants and divided among those three some of his possessions. To one man he gave five talents, representing a sizable sum of money. To another he gave two talents. To a third he gave one talent. Then the master left.

While he was gone, the man who was given five talents invested wisely and earned five more. The man given two talents did the same and earned two more. But the man who was given one talent buried it in the ground and did nothing with it.

The day of accounting came when the master returned and the three servants were called before him. He asked what they had done. The first and second stepped forward boldly, reporting how they had doubled the amount given. The master said, "Well done, thou good and faithful servant . . . enter thou into the joy of thy lord" (vv. 21,23).

The third servant, the one to whom just one talent was given, stepped forward to give his accounting to the master. He said, "Lord, I knew thee that thou art an hard man, reaping where thou has not sown, and gathering where thou has not strawed: And I was afraid, and went and hid thy talent in the earth: lo, there thou hast that is thine" (vv. 24-25). The master called this man a "wicked and slothful servant" (v. 26). Two servants acted in faith, believing they could do something with what they had been given; and they did. One servant decided in fear, and the decision he made was the wrong one.

Dr. B. H. Carroll gave good advice to George W. Truett at the beginning of his ministry. Dr. Carroll said to George Truett: "Young man, never take counsel of your fears." When you must decide, be sure your decision is governed by faith and not fears.

When you must decide, make sure your decision is:

Governed by Reason, Not Reaction

Gideon's initial reaction to the call was all wrong. First, when the Lord spoke to him about his concern for Israel, Gideon answered, "Oh my Lord, if the Lord be with us, why then is all this befallen us? and where be all his miracles which our fathers told us of, saying, Did not the Lord bring us up from Egypt? but now the Lord hath forsaken us, and delivered us into the hands of the Midianites" (Judg. 6:13). When the angel said the Lord was about to do something for Israel, Gideon reacted wrongly. He said in essence, "God doesn't care. If he did we wouldn't be in the mess we are in. He has cast us off; he has forsaken us."

When the Lord answered, "Gideon, not only am I going to do something, but I intend to use you in doing it," Gideon replied, "Oh my Lord, wherewith shall I save Israel? behold, my family is poor in Manasseh, and I am the least in my father's house" (v. 15). Again Gideon reacted wrongly. He said in essence, "If you are going to do something, you have certainly come to the wrong place to find somebody through whom you can work. My family are nobodies, and I am the least of the nobodies in my family."

The crisis of choice can cause one to react contrary to common sense. Someone has observed that there is nothing more uncommon in today's world than common sense. In stress situations a person can easily react rather than act. I am not trying to split semantical hairs when I talk about reacting and acting, for there is a vast difference between the two. To react is to do something because of what has happened. It is to respond to a stimulus. But to act is to do on the basis of individual choice. It is something done pursuant to one's volitional powers.

Far too many times people react rather than act, and in their reacting they become the losers. A good biblical example of the difference between acting and reacting can be found in the experience of Joseph and his brothers. Those brothers recognized that Joseph was the favorite son of their father, Jacob. They did not create that situation of favoritism, and they certainly did not like it. But they reacted to it by their jealousy toward Joseph. In their reaction they sold Joseph into slavery. Joseph's brothers were reactors, but Joseph was an actor. He ended up in Egypt as a slave. Rather than react to the difficulties of life which he did not choose, and for which he was hardly responsible, he decided to act and make the very best of a bad situation. Because he was an actor, he was a winner. He became the prime minister of Egypt.

The Lord calls people to decide on the basis of reason and not reaction. Reason dictated that the Lord was not against Israel. Since he called Gideon to service, he could certainly make the man equal to the task to which he was called.

Throughout the Scriptures God calls men to be reasonable and to decide on the basis of reason, not on the basis of reaction. Through Isaiah God spoke to a nation who had turned their backs upon him and walked in the counsel of the ungodly, stood in the way of sinners, and sat in the seat of the scornful. To that nation God said, "Come now, and let us reason together, saith the Lord: though your sins be as scarlet, they shall be white as snow; though they be red like crimson, they shall be as wool" (Isa. 1:18).

The Lord Christ gave us the pattern of acting reasonably and not in a reactionary fashion. When Jesus was opposed by the authorities of his day, he did not react to those who opposed him. Instead, he acted to do God's will. When you must decide, make certain your decision is governed by reason and not reaction.

And when you must decide, make sure your decision is:

Governed by Providence, Not Propaganda

Many decisions are based on false information. Gideon initially discredited the Lord's intention to deliver, thinking instead that the Lord had abandoned Israel and turned his back on his people. It is not specifically stated in the text, but I believe that Gideon was just repeating what he had heard others say. Men discussed the plight of the people in the marketplace during the day and around the fire at night. Gideon doubtless heard more than once, "God has abandoned us; God has forsaken us; God doesn't care about us. Look at our predicament. If God really did care, he would not have let this happen." When the angel of the Lord came and announced that the Lord was about to do something for Israel, Gideon simply repeated the propaganda he had heard.

The French critic Venet wrote: "Most friends of truth love it as Fredrick the Great loved music. It used to be said of him that, strictly speaking, he was not fond of music but of the flute, and not indeed fond of the flute but of his flute."[1]

It is so easy to give misleading information which can prompt the wrong decision and lead men to the wrong conclusion. The captain of a ship had a first mate who was addicted to alcohol. One day the first mate became drunk. He was discovered by the captain, who wrote into the log of the ship for that day this entry: "The first mate was drunk today." When the first mate sobered up and went on watch, he read what the captain had written. Recognizing that this could be a black mark against his record and a hindrance in getting a promotion, he went to the captain and asked him to delete the entry in the log.

The captain responded, "What I've written, I've written. It stays." The first mate went back to the bridge and wrote this entry in the log: "The captain was sober today." Anyone reading that might conclude that it was unusual for the captain to be sober. It is so easy to take something and twist it to make it sound as if it were something entirely different.

The right decision must be guided by God, not the words of men. Gideon asked for proof that the Lord had called him, and it was given. Therefore he decided to do what the Lord commanded him to do. His decision was not based upon propaganda—or what everyone said about God. His decision was based upon providence—what God led him to do.

The Lord is able to guide men in the stress situations of decision. The writer of the Proverbs was doubtless writing from experience when he said: "Trust in the Lord with all thine heart; and lean not unto thine own understanding. In all thy ways acknowledge him, and he shall direct thy paths" (3:5-6).

When one decides on the basis of propaganda, he can decide wrongly. The Lord God will never lead you to do wrong.

Conclusion

Life carries with it daily experiences of deciding. The greater the decision, the greater the stress factor in the decision. And the greater the stress factor in the decision, the greater the possibility of deciding wrongly. Some decisions are made once, never to be faced again. Others confront us as regularly as the birth of a new day. One cannot live without making decisions. Therefore, remember these principles when you must decide. Let your decision be governed by faith, not fears. Make your decision governed by reason, not reaction. Be sure your decision is governed by providence, not propaganda.

7
The Difficulties of Life

What does a millionaire Wall Street banker have in common with a homeless hobo whose only assets are the ragged clothes on his body? What does a society matron whose picture and name grace the woman's section of the Sunday newspaper have in common with a lonely widow forlorn, forsaken, and forgotten by society? There is a common denominator in the lives of these people, and it is trouble.

Job was overly pessimistic when, in the midst of the vicissitudes of his life, he said, "Man that is born of a woman is of few days, and full of trouble" (14:1, RSV). Overlooking the extreme pessimism of this man overwhelmed by his suffering, one does recognize the truth that trouble is a reality of every life. A good husband has been defined as one who stands by his wife in all the trouble she would never have had if she had not married him. The fact is that trouble is the common experience of all men. It is one of life's universals.

In living toward a vision we must learn how to cope with the troubles of life. Some help can be found for this essential learning process by considering the experiences of Joseph. I do not know a man in Scripture who was more victorious in facing and dealing with the difficulties, disappointments, and defeats of life. Consider the suffering he experienced, the steadfastness he exemplified, and the spirit he expressed.

The Suffering Experienced

While teaching in a Bible conference, I went to the host pastor's study during a break. There was a large diploma on one wall which caught my eye. With words written in beautiful script, the diploma announced that the pastor of that church was the recipient of a doctorate from the school of hard knocks. Many people have earned this degree. Joseph certainly was deserving of such an award, for he did postgraduate work in the school of hard knocks.

Consider these facts about Joseph's experiences. First, his brothers plotted to kill him and then settled on the plan to sell him into slavery. Thus Joseph's freedom was taken from him in an act of betrayal on the part of his own brothers (Gen. 37:25-28). Second, Joseph was falsely accused by a sensual and scheming woman. Serving as a slave in the house of Potiphar, Joseph became the object of Potiphar's wife's desires. When her advances were rejected she accused the youth of assaulting her (Gen. 39:17-18). Third, Joseph was forgotten by a man whom he befriended while in prison. Joseph asked the pharaoh's butler to remember him to the pharaoh when the butler was released. But for two years the butler forgot about the man who had befriended him (Gen. 40:23). Trouble followed trouble in Joseph's life. He knew experiences of heartache and disappointment.

A person does not live long in this world before he comes face to face with the reality of trouble. Suffering is a part of life, and one cannot evade the hard knocks which it brings. We are all enrolled as students in the school of hard knocks, and each day we attend classes in this school whose colors are black and blue.

Joseph learned some lessons about suffering. It is possible to delineate three lessons he learned from his experiences. Joseph learned that suffering can be the result of a person's own conduct. The other sons of Jacob were jealous of Joseph because he was obviously the favorite of their father. Joseph was not responsible for the favoritism shown him by Jacob. He did not do anything to cause his father to favor him over the other sons. Favoritism was shown Joseph because he was the son of Jacob's favorite wife, Rachel. However, even though Joseph was not responsible for Jacob's favoritism, he did flaunt it before his brothers. Joseph had a dream in which he was shown that he would have superiority over his brothers. He related that dream to his brothers when he awoke (Gen. 37:5-8). He would have been wise to have kept the dream to himself, for the telling of it caused them to hate him even more. Joseph's act of telling the dream pushed the brothers closer to their conduct of betrayal. When Joseph went to his brothers the day they sold him into slavery, they said, "Behold, this dreamer cometh" (Gen. 37:19). Joseph learned that a man can suffer as a result of his own conduct.

People often play the "blame game" when facing life's troubles. Other folks and situations are blamed for the trouble. However, many of life's troubles are experienced because of foolish and faulty conduct. In the final analysis, we are to blame for a lot of our own difficulties and dilemmas.

Second, Joseph learned that suffering can be the result of the evil deeds of others. He became a slave in Egypt because his brothers betrayed him. He was later thrown into prison because Potiphar's wife falsely accused him.

We live in a world where evil men operate. A person frequently experiences suffering as a result of what someone else does. Men with evil designs start wars in which thousands of innocent people suffer and die. Wicked men commit crimes of violence in which innocent people are the victims. Suffering is often the consequence of the actions of others.

Finally, Joseph learned that suffering can also be experienced in spite of faithfulness. The young man was faithful to God and what was right when Potiphar's wife made her amorous advances, endeavoring to seduce him (Gen. 39:7-10). He steadfastly refused to succumb to her enticements to evil. Frustrated in her desire, she finally accused Joseph of doing what he had refused to do. As a result he was put in prison (vv. 11-20). He suffered in spite of the fact that he remained faithful to God, the man who trusted him, and to himself. The Christian soon learns the truth that the Lord God does not build an impenetrable wall of security around him, making him immune to life's hurts.

Some of the most dedicated and faithful believers have known great suffering. One of the greatest cases in point is the apostle Paul. In 2 Corinthians 11:23-27 he gave a resumé of the difficulties and sufferings he experienced. Five times he was given thirtynine stripes with the whip; three times he was beaten with rods; he was stoned once; he was shipwrecked three times; and he lived in constant peril. All of this happened despite his faithfulness in serving God.

The Steadfastness Exemplified

Joseph was steadfast in hard times because he was equipped to deal with difficulty. There were several factors which served him well in the trying times. First, there was the training of his youth. Joseph was just seventeen years old when his brothers sold him into slavery. However, the strength of his character in troubling times indicates that he had been trained to do what was right. Even though Jacob's conduct usually left much to be desired, he apparently dedicated himself to training Joseph.

A second factor which helped Joseph to remain steadfast was

that he had a sense of direction in life. The Lord gave Joseph a dream in which the lad was given insight into his future (Gen. 37:5-10). Joseph lived with the daily consciousness that the Lord had something great in store for him. In the darkest nights of his life he was mindful of the bright star of his destiny. Added to these two factors was the commitment Joseph had to the Lord God. In the face of Potiphar's wife's seductive demands, Joseph asked, "How then can I do this great wickedness, and sin against God?" (Gen. 39:9). He recognized that God's law spoke about the conduct proposed and that to violate the law would be to sin against the Lord of the law.

A person needs anchors that will hold in the midst of the storms of life. He needs backup systems for life's difficulties. When our astronauts went into space and to the moon, they traveled in space capsules that contained backup systems. For each of the vital systems in the space ship there was a backup system. If the primary system failed, the backup system could be relied upon. Life can thrust us into situations in which one needs some backup systems.

Joseph was steadfast in difficulties, for he refused to give in. First, he did not give in and become bitter. How easy it would have been for Joseph to have become bitter toward those who had mistreated him! Personal injury can easily cause resentment; and resentment, once allowed to ferment, creates bitterness. This is the way in which many respond to being hurt. But Joseph refused to be resentful and thus did not become bitter. He was able to easily forgive his brothers years later because he had not nursed resentment and harbored bitterness in his heart.

Second, Joseph refused to give in to immorality. Both the temptation to sin and the opportunity to do so with the greatest of ease were very real. Potiphar's wife made herself most attractive to the young man and used all the wiles a woman knows to entice Joseph to respond to her. It would have been easy for Joseph to have judged sin with Potiphar's wife the reasonable thing to do. After all, she was his master's wife, and he was only a slave. Shouldn't a slave do what he was told? Doing what she asked would have given him the means to strike back. Further, what were the possibilities of exposure? How could he be caught? Potiphar's wife would be in no position to tell on him. Added to these reasons was the opportunity to satisfy the natural desires of his manhood. Yet Joseph steadfastly refused to give in to Potiphar's wife's enticements.

Men cannot escape the temptation to commit sin. James said it for all of us in the words "But every man is tempted" (Jas. 1:14). Being tempted does not mean that one must yield to the temptation. Some people seem to believe that temptation is sinful and that, since they are tempted, they may as well go on and sin. A young boy was going with some friends to the swimming hole. The boy's dad told him that he could go, but he could not go swimming.

When the boy returned home it was quite evident that he had gone swimming anyhow. When the father asked the boy why he disobeyed, he answered, "I was tempted to do it." The father then asked, "Why did you take your bathing suit?" The boy said, "I knew I was going to be tempted, so I wanted to be prepared." However, Joseph's story proves that a person can refuse the tempter and not give in to sin.

Third, Joseph would not give up and quit. One bruising blow followed another. He was betrayed by his brothers, falsely accused by his master's wife, forgotten by a man he had befriended. Joseph could easily have said, "What's the use? Why keep trying?" But he refused to give up. When his brothers sold him into slavery, he became the most faithful and diligent slave Potiphar had. When he was wrongly accused and thrown into prison, he did not retreat within himself to sulk and feel sorry for himself, but instead befriended others who needed help.

Joseph was steadfast in that he made the best of life situations. He had no choice in much that came to pass in his life, but he did have a choice about his own conduct when bad times came. Becoming a slave, he served Potiphar in such an exemplary manner that the captain made Joseph the steward of his house (Gen. 39:1-6). Joseph had no choice about becoming a slave, but he could choose what kind of slave he would be. When he was thrown into prison, Joseph responded to men in need and helped them (Gen. 40:21-23). He did not choose to spend years locked in a dungeon, but he could choose how he would use those years.

A person cannot always determine what will happen in life, but he can determine how he will act in life situations. It is within the power of every person to decide for himself whether the hard times of life will be allowed to break him or become the means for making a better life. What happens to a person is not nearly as important as how he reacts to it. Joseph took the difficult days of life and made the best of them. The difficulties of life were not allowed to become experiences of defeat but the stepping-stones to greatness.

The Spirit Expressed

Joseph refused to get revenge against those who had wronged him. The opportunity to get revenge came to Joseph. The pharaoh had a dream which none of his advisers could interpret. The butler remembered the man in prison who had explained his dream. When the pharaoh heard about Joseph, he sent for him. Joseph was able to interpret the king's dream. He capitalized on the situation and was made prime minister of Egypt (Gen. 41:1-45). Then came the day, twenty years after his brothers had sold him into slavery, that they came to stand before him as petitioners for bread (Gen. 42:1-8).

Other men who have been wronged by their fellowman have dreamed and prayed for an opportunity for revenge such as Joseph had. Joseph could have gotten revenge with impunity. He was second only to the pharaoh in power, and with a word he could have sent his brothers to prison, punishment, and death. Those brothers even expected him to get his revenge after Jacob died (Gen. 50:15). However, Joseph had not lived those twenty years with a heart filled with resentment and bitterness; thus he had no desire for revenge. Joseph's answer to their concern shows the spirit of the man. He asked, "Am I in the place of God?" (Gen. 50:19). Joseph was saying that settling scores was God's work, not his to do.

Getting even and getting back is something many people try to do. Revenge figures prominently in the plot of some novels and movies, for it has been the purpose of some men. Roger Chillingsworth in *The Scarlet Letter* and Edmond Dantès in *The Count of Monte Cristo* are classic examples of men who lived for revenge. Haman, who felt slighted by Mordecai, made revenge the sole object of his life. He was so intent on getting even with one man that he was willing to make thousands of innocent people suffer. His quest for revenge led to his own death, however. "So they hanged Haman on the gallows that he had prepared for Mordecai" (Esther 7:10). The Bible speaks explicitly against getting revenge. Centuries after Joseph, Paul wrote, "Repay no one evil for evil," and "Beloved, never avenge yourselves, but leave it to the wrath of God; for it is written, 'Vengeance is mine, I will repay, says the Lord' "(Rom. 12:17,19, RSV). Long before the apostle wrote these words Joseph put them into practice.

Not only did Joseph refuse to get revenge; he also practiced

Christian forgiveness. When he finally identified himself to his brothers, he comforted them with the words, "Now therefore be not grieved, nor angry with yourselves, that ye sold me hither" (Gen. 45:5). After Jacob's death the brothers, fearing Joseph would then get his revenge, sent a messenger to ask forgiveness. The messenger said, "Thy father did command before he died, saying, So shall ye say unto Joseph, Forgive, I pray thee now, the trespass of thy brethren, and their sin; for they did unto thee evil: and now, we pray thee, forgive the trespass of the servants of the God of thy father" (Gen. 50:16-17). The plea so touched Joseph that he broke down and wept. Again Joseph "comforted them and spake kindly unto them" (v. 21).

It is one thing to refuse to seek revenge against a person who did you an injustice, and an entirely different thing to forgive that person. Some people will not try to get revenge, but neither will they forgive. Joseph, who was done a great injustice by his brothers, was willing to forgive them. He covered the past with the blanket of forgiving love.

The Lord Christ taught that men are to forgive (Matt. 18:21-35). He said that one cannot be forgiven unless he is willing to forgive. Paul added that Christians are to forgive "one another, even as God for Christ's sake hath forgiven you" (Eph. 4:32). Beyond a doubt, this is one of the most difficult actions of life. This is especially true when the injury done was great with lasting consequences. But perhaps we will be more willing to forgive others if we stop and remember that no person has ever wronged us to the degree that we have sinned against God. And yet the Lord is ready to forgive. Dare we be any different?

Joseph was one of the most Christlike men in the Old Testament. A person is never more like God than when he responds in forgiveness to a guilty party, for this is how the Lord God responds to us.

Conclusion

Margaret Blair Johnson in her book *When God Says No* told of three lessons for life she learned in family experiences which were difficult and dangerous. The lessons were don't let go, don't run, and don't quit. These three lessons are evident in the experience of Joseph. He held on to his integrity, refused to play the role of the weakling, and exemplified steadfastness in spite of the most distressing difficulties.

Trouble is one of life's common denominators. Each person must learn how to deal with this reality of life. Joseph attended the school of hard knocks and was an honor graduate. As he faced the difficult experiences of life, he learned lessons and set an example which will serve us well as we live toward the vision of the Christ-life.

8
The Disappointments of Life

In the popular musical *My Fair Lady* Professor Henry Higgins exclaims, "I'm an ordinary man who desires nothing more than just the ordinary chance to live exactly as he likes and do precisely what he wants." There are many people who would breathe a fervent amen to that desire. It is the wish of many people, perhaps even yours, to live as they like and do what they want. But life does not always allow that. We are often disappointed in our desires.

Disappointments are realities of life. They often lead men to become disillusioned and even drop to the depths of despair. One person gave expression to his disappointment in the song:

> I'm waiting for ships that never come in,
> Watching and waiting in vain.
> It seems that life's stormy sea holds nothing for me,
> but broken dreams and golden schemes.
> With each day of sorrow I like to pretend,
> Some glad tomorrow the waiting will end.
> I'm waiting for ships that never come in,
> Watching and waiting in vain.[1]

The disappointments of life can be the result of many factors. Sometimes we experience disappointment because we expect too much. Disappointment can be the result of the conduct of others. All of us have known disappointment because of what someone did or did not do. How disappointed Barnabas must have been when John Mark left the mission team and went home to Jerusalem (Acts 13:13). Disappointment is also the consequence of failing in some plan or project.

We experience disappointments in living toward the vision of the Christ-life. If we are not careful, those disappointments in self, others, or circumstances can cause us to lose sight of the vision. Therefore, it is important that we learn how to deal with disappointments. I believe we can find some help through understanding an experience in the ministry of Paul.

Paul and Silas formed a mission team and set out from Antioch in Syria (Acts 15:40-41). Their initial destination was the area of Galatia, where Paul and Barnabas had preached and established churches during the first mission enterprise. Paul's ultimate destination, however, was Ephesus. His plans to minister there were thwarted (Acts 16:6-10). That was a disappointment for Paul, but one in which he refused to be defeated. The result was an even greater opportunity. In this experience we can see the closed doors, the continued determination, and the challenging discovery.

The Closed Doors

Paul faced closed doors in his desire to share the gospel of Christ. He wanted to preach in Ephesus, the capital of the Roman province of Asia. I believe the apostle had the dream of going to Ephesus for a long time. As a native of Tarsus, Paul certainly knew about the greatness of Ephesus. The desire to proclaim the gospel there may have been born in his heart soon after he began to preach.

It is very possible that Ephesus was Paul's intended destination on his first missionary journey. Having departed from Antioch in Syria and preached in Cyprus, Paul and his team landed in

Perga (Acts 13:4-13). From there they could easily have taken
a land route to Ephesus. However, Paul became ill and for health
reasons had to go into the highlands of central Turkey. Thus
it was that he and Barnabas preached in Galatia. When the apostle wrote to the Galatians, he reminded them that sickness had
furnished the occasion of his preaching to them (Gal. 4:13-14).
Galatia may not have been his intended goal. It may well have
been Ephesus.

There is no doubt that Paul was heading to Ephesus when
he and Silas set out on the second journey. Having visited the
new churches in Galatia (Acts 16:1-5), Paul headed straight for
Ephesus. But again the apostle was disappointed. The Bible says
he was "kept by the Holy Spirit from preaching the word in
the province of Asia" (Acts 16:6, NIV).

Thwarted in his desire to go to Ephesus, Paul turned north-
ward toward the prosperous Roman province of Bithynia on
the Black Sea. But again he experienced disappointment. "They
tried to enter Bithynia, but the Spirit of Jesus would not allow
them to" (v. 7, NIV).

It is my conviction that we do not read these verses rightly
unless we see in them a disappointed preacher. Paul came face
to face with two closed doors representing thwarted dreams
and blocked plans. Like anyone else, Paul must have been disappointed.

We, too, come face to face with disappointments. Roger Crook
in his book *How to Be Nervous and Enjoy It* says that there are
two kinds of disappointment. First, there is the disappointment
of hopes and dreams that never materialize. This was the type
of disappointment Paul experienced. He had dreamed of going
to Ephesus for so long, yet he was disappointed because the
dream did not become a reality. Second, there is the disappointment which comes because of unrealistic expectations. There

are times when we reach for unreachable stars. The failure we experience is born out of the folly of expecting too much.[2]

George Washington wrote a letter to his granddaughter Eliza in which he said: "There is no truth more certain than that our enjoyments fall short of our expectations." I take exception with Washington's statement, for I have known experiences when the enjoyment far exceeded the expectation. But I must agree with him that there are times when we can expect too much. Because of unrealistic expectations we are led to the experience of disappointment.

There is an interesting statement in 1 Kings 22:48 about King Jehoshaphat of Judah. The Bible says that Jehoshaphat built a fleet of cargo vessels with the purpose of sending them out to import gold. But those ships never sailed; they never left port. There are times when our dreams and hopes are like those ships—they never materialize into reality. All of us have faced the closed doors of disappointments.

The Continued Determination

Paul refused to be defeated by his disappointment. Even though the doors were closed to Asia and Bithynia, Paul kept on moving forward. There were two things the apostle refused to do. First, on facing the closed door of disappointment, he did not turn around and return to Antioch in Syria, saying, "The mission is a failure." Second, he did not sit down in front of those closed doors of disappointment and wallow in self-pity, lamenting the fact that he could not "live exactly as he liked and do precisely what he wanted."

Instead, the apostle kept moving forward. I am sure he believed that if the Lord did not want him to go to Ephesus or serve in Bithynia, he did have some place where he needed him. Paul knew that that place was not behind him, so he kept going forward. He refused to let his disappointment defeat him in his desire to serve.

Disappointments do not have to be the prelude to defeat. Yet that is often the case. In the midst of disappointment it is so easy to say, "What's the use? Why should I keep on trying?" or "Since I could not do what I wanted to do, why should I try something else?"

Disappointment can easily lead to discouragement. To be discouraged means to lose spirit and hope. Discouragement can, if allowed, lead to disillusionment. And disillusionment can lead to despair, causing one to give up and quit. The classic case of this deadly chain reaction which begins with disappointment is found in 1 Kings 18—19. Elijah was God's prophet who challenged the priests of Baal to a contest on Mount Carmel. The Lord answered by fire, and the priests of Baal were defeated. Elijah's victory was incomplete, for Jezebel threatened his life.

The prophet ran all the way to Beer-sheba, the southern boundary of Judah, then went a day's journey into the wilderness. He sat down under a tree, wallowing in self-pity, and wished to die. He said, "It is enough; now, O Lord, take away my life; for I am not better than my fathers" (1 Kings 19:4). It is possible to see the chain reaction of disappointment leading to discouragement, prompting disillusionment, and resulting in despair.

But disappointment does not have to mean defeat. It did not for Paul, who continued on in the face of disappointment. And it does not for you.

There are three very practical and helpful activities for the disappointing times in life. First, *accept* the fact. So many times people are unwilling to accept their disappointments. Many folks try to run away and pretend that all is well. Others attempt to escape in alcohol or other forms of drugs rather than face and accept life's disappointments. It is necessary to accept the fact that you face a closed door, for until you do you cannot take the next two steps.

Second, *alter* your plans. After all, disappointment does not mean that all possibilities are out of the question. It means that one possible course of action is not workable at that time. There are other things to do instead. When Paul found the doors to Asia and Bithynia closed, he did not take it to mean that there were no open doors anywhere. Instead, he resolutely moved on, altering his plans as he sought another place of service.

Third, *attempt* something else. I have discovered that one of the best medicines for disappointment is to get busy doing something else. Sir Walter Scott wanted to be a poet. He tried to write poetry and failed. As a second choice he began to write novels. But Scott was so ashamed of his first novels that he had them published anonymously. This man who failed to become a poet and in his disappointment began to write novels was called the king of romantics by Robert Louis Stevenson.

James Whistler was a cadet at the Military Academy at West Point. He wanted to become an army officer. But he flunked out of the academy because he failed chemistry. His dreams of army service ended in disappointment. However, Whistler became a great artist instead. His painting of *The Artist's Mother* is famous in the world of art. Paul responded to his disappointment by attempting to serve wherever God would open the door.

The Challenging Discovery

The apostle Paul found a greater opportunity for service as a result of disappointment than he would have had the doors to Asia and Bithynia not been closed. Paul and his team continued on to Troas. Luke wrote, "And they passing by Mysia came down to Troas" (Acts 16:8). Notice, Luke said "down" to Troas. Perhaps he was expressing something of the topography of the area. Paul and his company were coming from the highlands of the interior down to the seacoast city of Troas. But there is a significant message in that statement. Troas was a comedown for Paul. He had not intended to go there. Troas could not offer the opportunities of Ephesus or Bithynia. But it was the only place left to go, so Paul "came down to Troas."

It was in Troas, however, that the apostle had the vision of the man of Macedonia calling out, "Come over into Macedonia, and help us" (Acts 16:9). Paul took that call to be God's revelation of his will about where he was to serve. The Lord who had closed the doors to Ephesus and Bithynia opened the door to Macedonia.

The apostle moved through that open door and discovered opportunities for service he had not dreamed of. Churches were established in Philippi, Thessalonica, Berea, and Corinth. It should be noted that Paul's favorite church was located in Philippi. The letter to the Philippians reveals a bond of love between Paul and that church stronger than any that existed anywhere else. A relationship was established between the preacher and the people in Philippi which neither years nor distance could diminish. That precious relationship was a result of Paul's disappointment over Asia.

Some of the greatest discoveries and dividends in life come in the wake of some of our greatest disappointments. A star is one of the most beautiful sights in this physical universe. On clear nights I look up at the stars, and they seem to be diamonds sparkling in the sky. But you cannot see the stars until it gets dark. You cannot see them in the sunlight. So it is that in the darkness of disappointment we can often discover priceless diamonds.

The Bible and life furnish abundant examples of people who discovered opportunities in the midst of disappointment. Isaiah was a young man in the kingdom of Judah. He may have been of royal birth and a relative of the king. He certainly had access to the royal court. But one day the only king he had known in his lifetime died. Uzziah, who had ruled Judah for fifty-two years, was dead; and he died a leper. Crushed by that experience, Isaiah went to the house of God. There, in that dark night of disappointment and discouragement, he met the Lord (Isa. 6:1-9). In his discouragement over the death of King Uzziah, Isaiah met the King of kings who never dics!

Jacob loved Rachel so much that he willingly worked seven years to win her hand in marriage. But on his wedding night his father-in-law, Laban, tricked him and gave him Leah instead of Rachel. Leah was the older, weak-eyed, and not-so-beautiful sister of Rachel. Jacob had to work seven more years to have Rachel as well. But it just may be that Leah was the better wife. She was certainly the one by whom he fathered Judah, who was in the lineage of Christ. Thus there was a dividend from his disappointment.

As a young man George Washington had the desire to go to sea as a cadet in the navy of King George of England. He had his trunk packed and his passage paid on a ship to transport him from America to England. At the last minute his plans were thwarted. Instead of going to England to become an officer in the king's navy, George Washington eventually became a general in the Continental Army and the first president of the newly formed republic.

Years ago there lived in Decatur, Illinois, a boy who was deeply interested in photography. He saved his money in order to purchase a particular book on photography. When he had enough money he ordered the book. But a mistake was made at the mail-order house. Instead of their sending the boy the desired book on photography, a book on ventriloquism was sent. At the time the boy did not even know what ventriloquism was. Neither did he know that he could return the book and request that the mistake be corrected. In his disappointment he could have put the unwanted book on ventriloquism aside. Instead, he began to read it and became interested. He learned how to throw his voice. In time he bought several dummies, the most famous of which he named Charlie McCarthy. Out of his disappointment Edgar Bergen became nationally famous as a ventriloquist and as a popular entertainer who delighted millions.

Dover, England, was heavily bombed by the Germans during World War II. A resident of that city had a garden in his backyard which was a well-known attraction. During an air raid a German bomb fell in that beautiful garden, leaving a crater ten feet deep and twenty feet across. The gardener discovered an opportunity in that disappointment. He smoothed and shaped the bomb crater and made a beautiful sunken garden out of it.

Like Paul, Isaiah, Jacob, Washington, Bergen, and a host of others, we, too, can make some challenging discoveries in the midst of some of our greatest disappointments.

Conclusion

With Professor Henry Higgins in *My Fair Lady*, we often desire nothing more than the chance to live exactly as we like and do precisely what we want. Yet we are usually disappointed in that desire.

The experience of Paul can teach us a valuable lesson for the disappointments of life. Like us, he, too, faced closed doors representing disappointment. Instead of allowing these to defeat

THE DISAPPOINTMENTS OF LIFE

him and giving in to self-pity, Paul continued in his desire to find a place of service. Because of that determination, he made a challenging discovery which led to the finding of great opportunities. We can do the same when disappointments darken our skies.

9

The Domestication of Life

The Bible teaches that man was created for relationships. Interestingly, the first question man asked that is recorded in the Bible was not a question about theology or the universe, or even about how man came to be. It was a question dealing with relationships. Cain asked, "Am I supposed to take care of my brother?" (Gen. 4:9, TEV).

Obviously and primarily, the Lord God created man for relationship with the Creator and Sustainer. Salvation reduced to its simplest definition is a relationship with the living God. That relationship is entered into by faith in Jesus Christ, and it is one in which the believer is to grow and develop. No man has achieved his purpose in being born and having the gift of physical life until he comes to share life in a relationship with the Lord.

Man was also created for a relationship with other persons. The book of Genesis teaches that the Lord God saw that it was not good for man to be alone; therefore, he made a companion for the man. The Lord brought the woman to the man and led the two into a life relationship. This interaction of lives is called marriage.

Domestication is one of life's greatest challenges. And yet, tragically, it is a challenge in which man so often fails. This is not only true today; it has been true across the centuries.

Through the Word of God a person gains insights into the lives and marriages of some of the great people who walked across the stage of divine revelation. This insight into those marriages reveals that in many cases the relationships were marred by mistakes and faded because of failure. The same is true today. In spite of the fact that most bookstores stock scores of books which deal with making a marriage, people continue to fail in this challenge of life.

In living toward the vision of the life in Christ, one must give attention to the domestic side of life. How wrong the churchman was who said that his marriage relationship and home life had no relation to his spiritual journey of faith!

The experience of Adam and Eve furnishes us some biblical insights into making a marriage and the domestication of life. Obviously, their relationship does not give us a step-by-step blueprint on how we can make a marriage which will be without failures or mistakes. However, this relationship does furnish some helpful insights.

The Dream in Marriage

Adam and Eve enjoyed a perfect marriage for a time. After all, how could their marriage have been anything but perfect? Genesis tells us in chapter 1 that the Lord God acted creatively and that everything which now exists was brought into being by his creative powers. God spoke the world into being; he divided light and darkness; he created animal and botanical life; and he created man. Since the God who acted in creation is perfect, how could all he created be anything less than perfect? This was also true of man. Little wonder the Bible declares that when the Lord God finished creation and looked on all he had done, he saw that "it was very good" (Gen. 1:31).

Thus the first couple enjoyed a perfect marriage for a time.

They did so because they were a perfect pair, living in a perfect place, with a perfect purpose. Sociologists have grouped marriages today in five categories. These are the conflict-habituated, the devitalized, the passive-congenial, the vital, and the total marriage. Adam and Eve began life together experiencing a total marriage. It was a relationship and interaction of lives as God intended it to be.

Perfection in marriage is an impossible dream. The initial perfection Adam and Eve experienced in their marriage is impossible for couples today. People can have good marriages and good marriages can be made better, but perfection is out of the question. However, many young people have not learned that perfection is an impossible dream. We have created a storybook idea about life in which "some enchanted evening" two people see each other across a crowded room, are immediately attracted to each other, and fall in love as Cupid's arrow pierces their hearts. The couple then join their lives in the relationship called marriage, setting sail on the sea of matrimony, blissfully expecting to live happily ever after. Unfortunately, that is not the way it goes.

When I counsel with couples planning to be married, I try to make them aware of some of the problems they can expect to encounter. Though few couples actually say it aloud, many look at each other with starry eyes and smiling lips as if to say, "We know our folks' marriages are not perfect, for we know some problems they have; but it won't be that way with us." Some of these same couples are back in a few months or years seeking advice and help. They have been sobered by the reality that perfection in marriage is an impossible dream, for the two who make the marriage are not perfect.

A young husband of just two weeks said to his wife, "Honey, in these weeks we've been married, I've discovered some faults in you I didn't know you had. Would you mind if I pointed them out to you?" His bride smiled sweetly and responded, "No, dear. You go right ahead; but just remember that those are the same faults which kept me from getting a better husband than I did."

It would really be something if there were some knight in shining armor on whose gleaming coat there were no rust spots. It would be something if there were some fair young damsel, as flawless in character as in complexion. But if such existed and you found one for a mate, the result would be disastrous. Can you imagine what it would be like for a perfect man and an imperfect woman to be joined in marriage? Can you imagine how awful it would be for a perfect woman to have an imperfect man as her mate for life? Marriage is a relationship designed by God, but it is experienced by imperfect people. Those who recognize the imperfections of their own lives are willing to accept the imperfections in the lives of others. One woman expressed it this way:

> I hate a man who's never late;
> Whose every sock has got a mate;
> Who's never missed a single date,
> And never even tarried.
> Give me the man who's unaware,
> Who loses things; who's never there;
> And we will make a perfect pair.
> In fact, we do. We're married.

In the domestication of life, do not expect perfection. Adam and Eve experienced that in their relationship for a while, but no other couple can or does.

The Difficulties of Marriage

The first couple came to experience difficulties and problems in their marriage. This fact is revealed in that tragic passage, Genesis 3:1-7. Consider what happened to them and their union.

First, Eve came to want more than she had. The Lord's provisions were abundantly adequate, but Satan tempted the woman to want more. Eve found the fruit of the forbidden tree desirable.

A part of this tragedy is that in desiring what she did not need, she and her husband lost what they had. I have discovered that the practice of love can become a casualty to the pursuit of luxuries. There are many couples who are far more intent on getting the good things of life than they are upon enjoying the good life God has given. Trying to keep up with the Joneses can be very hard on a marital relationship.

Second, Eve not only desired what she did not need; she disobeyed God. The Lord God said that the tree of the knowledge of good and evil was off limits (Gen. 2:17). Eve disregarded God's warning and disobeyed God's command. It is not simplistic to say that problems are sure to come when a couple disregards God and disobeys his instructions. Sin not only separates men from God; it has a tremendous consequence in marriage.

Third, the Bible reveals that the first couple failed each other in their crisis of temptation and disobedience. Adam did not stop his wife in her act of disobedience. Where was he while Satan was dealing with Eve? Had Adam gone fishing? Had he slept late that day? Was he on a business trip to some other part of the garden? Adam failed Eve in that he did not provide the leadership she needed in the tempting time.

Furthermore, Eve failed Adam, for she exercised her influence over him in the wrong way. Eve gave some of the forbidden fruit to Adam. Satan did not tempt the man to sin. The woman influenced him to do so. One man said that Adam was disobedient because he wanted to share Eve's fate. The Lord God had said that if they ate the forbidden fruit, they would die. Eve ate and had the sentence of death upon her, so Adam also ate. I am a romantic soul, but I do not believe this was the reason for Adam's disobedience. Whatever the man's reason was, the fact remains that each failed the other. Their perfect relationship came to be one with difficulties and problems.

Marital difficulties are commonplace today. Numerous books are published which deal with the problems in marriage. The studies and surveys of marital dysfunctions are endless. One of the most recent surveys involved 750 professional marriage counselors. These people were asked to identify and rank in order of severity the greatest problems in marriage today. The difficulties identified were: (1) a breakdown in communication; (2) the loss of shared goals and interests; (3) sexual incompatibility; (4) infidelity; (5) the loss of fun and excitement in marriage; (6) money; (7) conflict over children; (8) alcohol and drugs; (9) women's equality issues; (10) in-laws.[1]

Dr. David Mace stated that marriages fail for only one reason—"because the persons involved have been unable to achieve mutual love and intimacy." He added that the various problems in marriage "are not the real causes of trouble. They are only the arenas in which the inner failure of the relationship becomes outwardly demonstrated."[2]

Many couples complicate and compound marital difficulties by doing the wrong things in dealing with them. The Bible shows that Adam and Eve reacted the wrong way when difficulty became a reality in their marriage relationship. The Scriptures say that they attempted a futile cover-up, then ran and tried to hide from God (Gen. 3:7-8). When the Bible says that their eyes were opened and they knew they were naked, it is not saying their nakedness was sinful. That condition of being naked had not been sinful before their disobedience (Gen. 2:25), and sin had not changed that. Rather, the meaning is that they had lost their state of innocence, and their shame was the giveaway that something had interfered with their intimacy and destroyed their innocence. However, the couple's reaction to their situation was wrong from start to finish. To run from God is the height of folly, and to attempt to cover up what makes one aware of a problem is the wrong way to solve the problem.

One of the greatest tragedies on the marital scene today is that many couples, who are experiencing difficulties and problems which interfere with intimacy and make the experience of mutual happiness in marriage impossible, choose to suffer in silence or to grin and bear it. Instead of seeking help from those qualified to offer directions, so many couples try to pretend that there is no problem and hide it behind some facade. One of the greatest heartaches I have experienced in the area of family counseling is to have couples come with problems which have been unattended for so long that their situation has become virtually incurable.

Difficulties in marriage are much like sickness. When a person who is sick takes the proper remedial action, the illness is arrested and a cure is experienced. But if the sickness is left unattended and untreated, it can become fatal. I do not know of a single marital problem which solves itself without some remedial action being taken. When the difficulties are left untreated, they can easily become fatal for the marriage.

The Directions for Marriage

Adam and Eve received directions for their marriage. Those instructions are recorded in Genesis 2:24. The Lord God designed the relationship of marriage; therefore, he is qualified to give directions about it. It is commonplace for a manufacturer to include a set of operational instructions with the product he produces. Who is better qualified to say how a particular machine or appliance is to be used in order to give maximum performance than the ones who designed and made it? Since marriage is a life relationship designed by God and not thought up by man, God is the one who has the right to say how it is to work.

It is often said that marriages are made in heaven. I take that to mean that the institution of marriage is divinely ordained. However, marriage can be described as a do-it-yourself project. It is put together on earth, which involves human factors.

When the Lord gave the first bride in marriage to the first bridegroom, he said, "Therefore a man leaves his father and his mother and cleaves to his wife, and they become one flesh" (Gen. 2:24, RSV). In that verse the Lord identified three activities which are vitally essential for the making of a marriage. These are leaving, cleaving, and achieving.

First, there must be a *leaving* of father and mother. A man was not to sever all connections with his parents; nor is a couple to do this today. A person is all of his life what he was on the first day of life—the child of his parents. The Bible makes it clear that children have responsibilities toward their parents and that marriage does not nullify these obligations.

The leaving involved in the directions God gave relates to priority and dependence. In marriage a relationship is established which must have priority over all other relationships among men. The only obligation which supersedes marriage is the relationship a person has with God. When my older daughter and her young man came to ask my permission to marry, I told them that they must love each other more than any other human beings—even their parents. It is not easy for a father to say to his daughter that she must love some other man more than she does him, but this is a part of the leaving process.

Furthermore, in the leaving of parents, the couple is not to be dependent on them. That includes financial as well as psychological dependence. It used to be that couples began life together in an apartment furnished in "early newlywed." It is common today for newlyweds to start out with a house or apartment furnished with the best due to the generosity of their parents, and their early years are undergirded with financial supplements. Certainly this is a contributor to in-law difficulties in marriage.

Second, God's directions state that there is to be a *cleaving*. In leaving father and mother, the man is to "cleave unto his wife." The word cleave in the Hebrew comes from the root meaning to join or to be glued together. Thus the idea in cleaving is the commitment of two lives to each other.

Marriage is basically a commitment of two people to each other. This is what happens in the marriage ceremony when the bride and groom make their vows to each other. My father once asked me at what point in the ceremony the two became married. He asked, "Is it when you pronounce them to be husband and wife?" My answer was that the couple became married the moment they pledged their lives to each other.

The lack of commitment is one of the faults I find with the popular "living together" arrangements today. Couples who opt for that should be honest and not call their arrangement a meaningful relationship. It cannot be that if it lacks the foundation of commitment. The commitment of cleaving is the glue which holds a relationship together.

Finally, God directed that marriage includes *achieving*. The man and his wife are to "become one flesh." The term "one flesh" has a number of implications, but it obviously refers to sexual relationships. The Hebrew word for flesh, *basar*, has a wide range of meaning. It speaks of "the fleshly substance of an animal body, the body itself, a human being, a blood relative, mankind, any mortal creature, the whole transient creation, the sexual organs. . . ."[3]

Even though "one flesh" refers to the physical relationship in marriage, it also implies a unity of emotions, minds, purpose, and attitudes which gives added meaning to intimacy. This unity also implied in the "one flesh" concept is not attained or achieved overnight. It is the end result of a becoming process. Thus, in marriage two people are to give themselves daily to the process of achieving the total intimacy expressed in the phrase "one flesh." There is nothing automatic or instantaneous about this.

Conclusion

Man was created for relationships. The idea of one person living alone without any companionship is untenable so far as the Bible is concerned. The state of being alone is dehumanizing, and solitary confinement is considered by some as the most inhumane form of punishment.

The Lord God created man for relationship with himself. Of all the creatures God made, only man has the capacity to know God. Furthermore, the Lord God saw man's need of relationship with one of his own kind. Thus, woman was created and the relationship of marriage was given.

The achievement of all God wills for a man and woman united in the relationship of marriage is not easily accomplished. It requires a lifetime of work. Success in the domestication of life demands realistic expectations, obedience to God's directions, and submission to the lordship of Christ.

10
The Declarations of Life

It is interesting to recognize how much of life is made up of words and the use of words. There are some 2,796 known languages and dialects in the world. Stop for a moment and realize how many words are involved in the English language alone. It takes a child several years to learn as many as 1,000 of those 700,000 words. In their lifetime some men become articulate enough to have at their command between 6,000 and 30,000 words. It is estimated by the statisticians that we speak at the average rate of 125 words per minute. Some speak slower and more deliberately than that, and some speak faster than that. I heard about a weather forecaster who said of his wife, "She speaks at the rate of 150 words a minute with gusts up to 190."

The Bible has much to say about words and the use of them. The psalmist said our words are to be acceptable in God's sight. "Let the words of my mouth and the meditation of my heart, be acceptable in thy sight, O Lord, my strength and my redeemer" (Ps. 19:14). Jesus said, "Men will render account for every careless word they utter" (Matt. 12:36, RSV). The psalmist said that the words of a hypocrite are "smoother than butter" and "softer than oil" (Ps. 55:21). "The words of the whisperer are like delicious morsels" (Prov. 18:8, RSV), and a man hasty in speech is worse than a fool (Prov. 29:20). Solomon said that a fool is known by his multitude of words (Eccl. 5:2).

Speaking is the most social thing the average person does. The way other people learn what we believe, feel, and think is by means of communication, most of which is verbal or written. This makes communication one of the most important things we do. It is also one of our biggest problems. More troubles are experienced by the average person because of things said than by things done. In living toward a vision, a person needs to recognize the importance of speech and learn the proper use of the tongue.

James dealt with practical religion in his brief epistle. He did not write from the vantage point of the ivy-covered tower of an academician, but stayed instead on the street level of everyday life. One aspect of that practical religion is the control of the tongue. In James 3:1-12 the apostle of practical Christianity had some pertinent things to say about this. What he wrote long ago sheds light on the declarations of life.

The Power of the Tongue

James stated that the tongue has power out of proportion to its small size. "Even so the tongue is a little member, and boasteth great things" (3:5). The writer illustrated the tongue's power in proportion to its size by referring to the bit in a horse's mouth and the rudder of a ship. Compared to the size of a horse, a bit is a very small piece of equipment. However, by using the bit, a rider can guide the horse in the direction he desires. The rudder of a ship is not very big when compared to the immense size of the hull and superstructure of the vessel. However, by using the rudder, the pilot of the ship can steer the vessel in the direction he desires. The bit and rudder are small objects with power greater than their size.

The tongue is a small member of the body. I have never weighed a tongue, but logic dictates that it does not weigh as much as a hand or foot. The tongue is a small part of the body, but it has a power out of proportion to its small size.

The writer of the Proverbs had a great deal to say about the tongue and the power of speech. One of his most piercing statements is, "Death and life are in the power of the tongue" (Prov. 18:21). He said that the tongue has the power to kill, or to give life. This truth was expressed by the unknown person who wrote the lines:

> A careless word may kindle strife,
> A cruel word may wreck a life.
> A bitter word may hate instill,
> A brutal word may smite and kill.
> A joyous word may smooth the way,
> A gracious word may lighten the day.
> A timely word may lessen stress,
> A loving word may heal and bless.

There is a collection of books in some Bibles called the Apocrypha. One of these books is Ecclesiasticus, containing the writings of Jesus ben Sirach. He wrote:

> Curses on the gossip and the tale-bearer! For they have been the ruin of many peaceable men./The talk of a third party has wrecked the lives of many/and driven them from country to country;/it has destroyed fortified towns/and demolished the houses of the great./The talk of a third party has brought divorce on staunch wives/and deprived them of all they have laboured for. Whoever pays heed to it will never again find rest/or live in peace of mind./The lash of a whip raises weals,/ but the lash of a tongue breaks bones./Many have been killed by the sword,/but not so many as by the tongue (28:13-18, NEB).

James focused on the destructive power of the tongue. He used the metaphors of fire and poison to illustrate this power.

He called the tongue a fire and said that the whole cycle of nature has been set on fire by the tongue, which is "set on fire by hell" (3:6). Fire has many good uses. It can warm your house, cook your food, and furnish energy for industry. But a fire out of control spells disaster. So it is with the tongue. Dr. Louis Evans wrote:

> One careless word tossed out of your mouth—and there is a fire. One lie, one sentence of gossip with the lift of an eyebrow, one hellish insinuation, one evil story—and the conflagration begins. Human hearts can be like tinder, dry of the milk of human kindness and parched for the lack of rains of mercy; in such tinder the holocaust comes quickly, leaping through hearts and homes, across towns, into newspaper columns and conversations, fanned by the winds of hatred and man's merciless depravity, until the smell of burned flesh, destroyed homes and scarred souls is everywhere—all because one tongue wagged out of control.[1]

Then James said that the tongue is like a poison. He called it "An unruly evil, full of deadly poison" (3:8). Paul said the same to the Romans when he described the ungodly. "Their throat is an open sepulchre; with their tongues they have used deceit; the poison of asps is under their lips" (Rom. 3:13). The bite of a poisonous snake can be deadly. The venom from a tongue can be equally deadly.

It is essential for us to be aware of the power of speech. To speak is to release energy. When speech gets out of control, the energy released can be very destructive.

The Perversions of the Tongue

Power can be perverted and used for destructive purposes. This is true of the power of speech and words. James wrote

that the tongue can become an instrument of evil. He called
the tongue "a world of iniquity" (3:6). J. B. Phillips translated
that statement "with vast potentialities for evil." [2] Curtis Vaughan wrote, "We might think of many wicked things the tongue
does, such as kindling lust, speaking blasphemy, stirring up
strife, dividing churches, embittering families." [3] Thus this
member of the body can be perverted.

The tongue is perverted when it is *foul*. Profanity and obscen-
ity have become commonplace in America. A form of perverted
speech has come to be accepted as normal. Nearly twenty years
ago L. Nelson Bell wrote, "We live in a time when profanity
is so universal that it arouses little comment and even less resentment. That this is, in part, an aftermath of two world wars is
no excuse. That many women are also guilty in no way lessens
its offensiveness or seriousness. In fact children now hear these
'crooked words' from many sources, including their own
homes."[4] What was true twenty years ago is truer today. On-
the-street talk, books, movies, television programs, political inter-
views, and conversations in the home are punctuated with four-
letter words and profane expressions.

A fifth grader was talking to his mother after school one afternoon. He used a word he had heard at school that day. His
mother said, "I'll give you a quarter if you'll never say that
word again." Several days later the boy said to his mother, "You
remember the word you gave me a quarter not to say?" When
she answered Yes, he said, "I heard one today worth a dollar!"

Many Americans were shocked by the repeated phrase "exple-
tive deleted" in the transcripts of the White House Watergate
tapes. But shock is fast being replaced by conditioning in which
there is greater acceptance and expression of foul talk. This
type of noise pollution is a perversion of the tongue.

The tongue is perverted when it is *ferocious*. James wrote about the taming of wild animals and then said, "But the tongue can no man tame; it is an unruly evil" (3:7-8). Like an untamed wild animal, the tongue can be a ferocious thing. It is ferocious when it is harsh and hard. People who never resort to physical violence are often experts at verbal violence.

The tongue is also ferocious when it is an instrument of gossip and slander. Gossip is usually a lie passed on surreptitiously, either for the dubious pleasure of creating a sensation or for the more overt intention of injuring the one who is the subject of it.

Jeremiah was not a popular preacher. He had his enemies, and they set about to do him in. "Then they said, 'Come, let us make plots against Jeremiah, for the law shall not perish from the priest, nor counsel from the wise, nor the word from the prophet. Come, let us smite him with the tongue, and let us not heed any of his words'" (Jer. 18:18, RSV).

Gossip is a commonplace sin today. Rare indeed is the person who is not guilty. It is one of the prevalent sins in Christian circles, and the outcome is usually ruined reputations and ruptured relations. The wise man of old wrote: "You can be ruined by the talk of godless people" and "Gossip is spread by wicked people; they stir up trouble and break up friendships" (Prov. 11:9; 16:28, TEV). Alexander Pope wrote:

> "The flying rumors gathered as they rolled,
> Scarce any tale was sooner heard than told;
> And all who told it added something new,
> And all who heard it made enlargements too,
> In every ear it spread, on ev'ry tongue it grew."[5]

The ancient Jews looked on gossip as a cardinal sin and defined it as "any rumor or report that would mar or defame the reputation of another human being."[6] That the Lord God despises the ferocious tongue of the gossiper and slanderer is clear in

Scripture. James wrote, "Do not criticize one another, my brothers. Whoever criticizes a Christian brother or judges him, criticizes the Law and judges it" (4:11, TEV).

The tragedy of the ferocious tongue is compounded by the fact that often the damage done by something said cannot be undone. How many times have we said something in the heat of anger or on an impulse of a moment, only to wish we could take it back? In counseling people about communication problems I advise them to take lightly some things said in anger, for many times this was the temper and not the heart speaking. But at the same time I remind them that once something is said, it cannot be recalled. A childhood rhyme by an unknown person reminds us:

> Boys, flying kites, pull in their white-winged birds,
> But this you cannot do, when you're flying words.
> Thoughts unexpressed may someday fall back dead.
> But God Himself cannot kill them when once they are said.

The tongue is perverted when it is *forked*. The Indians denounced the man who spoke with a forked tongue, and James wrote of good and bad words coming from the same mouth (3:9-12). He wrote of the man who speaks blessings to God and curses to men. Here is the fellow who praises God in heaven and tells his neighbor to go to hell.

Curtis Vaughan related the following episode: "A little girl sat with her arms wrapped around her father's neck. But her mother observed that over her father's shoulder she was sticking out her tongue at her little brother. The mother responded by saying, 'Take your arms from around your father's neck. You cannot love your father and at the same time stick out your tongue at his son.' To profess love for God while reviling men made in His image is a brazen offense against God."[7]

Paul, writing to Timothy about the qualifications of deacons, said that a deacon is not to be double-tongued (1 Tim. 3:8). That means that he is not to talk one way in one setting, and a different way in another setting. John Bunyan had a character named Talkative. He said about him, "He was a saint abroad but a devil at home." Such a forked tongue is perverted.

The Purpose of the Tongue

The Lord God gave us the ability of speech for good reasons. A naturalist once said that the one thing that distinguishes a man from beasts is the fact that a man can talk. Obviously there is a greater distinction between the two than that, for man was created in the image of God. And yet there is that difference— a man can talk. He has the ability to verbalize what he feels, thinks, and believes. He can escape isolation as he speaks to others who can hear and understand him.

One of the happiest moments for parents is when their infant speaks its first intelligible words. The parents can hardly wait to tell others. Of course, it isn't long until the parents are wishing he would be quiet sometimes. I think I belong to the left-out generation. When I was a child we were told that children were to be seen, not heard. Now that I am an adult I find myself in a youth-oriented society in which I am told to be quiet and listen to youth. I wonder when I'll get my chance to speak!

What a blessing it is to be able to speak. We can speak our love to the significant other in our lives. We can share our hopes and dreams. We can talk of our beliefs and doubts. The gift of speech is a wonderful blessing which God gave to us for good reasons.

Speech was given to us for the purpose of *counsel*. My life has been enriched by words of counsel spoken to me by others. In the classroom, in a time when I needed direction or correction, in a period of crisis, someone wiser and more experienced spoke words of counsel. This is one of the good purposes of the tongue.

The tongue has the purpose of speaking *commendation*. How quick we are to criticize and condemn others, yet how slow to express appreciation. It takes so little effort to say a simple "thank you" or to tell someone that we appreciate what he did. How much brighter we can make another person's day by speaking a word of commendation. Tragically, we often wait until it's too late to do this.

Is there someone you need to speak an encouraging word to? Perhaps you feel gratitude or appreciation for the person. How will he know unless you tell him? This is a good purpose of the tongue.

Furthermore, God gave us the tongue for the purpose of *confession*. Man is to confess faith in Jesus Christ as Savior. Paul said, "That if you confess with your mouth, 'Jesus is Lord,' and believe in your heart that God raised Him from the dead, you will be saved. For it is with your heart that you believe and are justified, and it is with your mouth that you confess and are saved" (Rom. 10:9-10, NIV). Jesus said, "Whosoever therefore shall confess me before men, him will I confess also before my Father which is in heaven" (Matt. 10:32).

Not only is the tongue to confess your faith in Christ; it is also to share your faith in Christ with other people. The psalmist said, "Let the redeemed of the Lord say so, whom he hath redeemed from the hand of the enemy" (Ps. 107:2) and "Come and hear, all you who fear God, /and I will tell what he has done for me" (Ps. 66:16, RSV). Failing to speak to others about Christ is as great a sin as using the tongue for blasphemy or deceit.

With the tongue we can share the best news any man can hear—the news that God loves all men and gave himself in Christ for our salvation. The Bible says that the name of Jesus Christ was magnified in the city of Ephesus during Paul's ministry there (Acts 19:17). This was done as people talked about Jesus.

Conclusion

God has given us the ability to speak. This is a blessing with a corresponding responsibility. It is a gift not to be misused.

Hugh Latimer was a great English preacher in another generation. One day he was in the chapel where he frequently preached when the King of England came in to take his seat as a member of the congregation. Hugh Latimer walked to the pulpit to deliver his sermon. Recognizing the presence of the King of England, he said aloud, "Latimer, watch what thou sayest; thy king heareth thee." Then he stepped to the right of the pulpit and cried a little louder, "Watch what thou sayest, Latimer, thy king heareth thee." Then he stepped to the left of the pulpit and shouted, "Latimer, Latimer, watch what thou sayest; thy king heareth thee." Friend, watch what you say. The King of kings hears you.

11
The Dividends of Life

A psychologist took a group of 142 ministers, priests, and rabbis and asked them to answer the question "What does it mean to be religious?" The answers given by the clergymen were arranged in five categories. First, some clergymen equated being religious with rituals, creeds, and traditions. Second, there were those who said that being religious meant having a high degree of morality. They said that a religious person does not smoke, drink, curse, etc. Third, there were some clerics who said that being religious meant to be involved in social causes which help the underprivileged. Fourth, some said being religious meant having faith in God.

Last, there were those who answered the question by saying that it means to participate in church programs and activities. That last group thought of being religious in terms of doing religious things such as praying, singing, giving, and the like. They were like the deacon who was a passenger on a transatlantic flight. The plane developed engine trouble and began descending toward the stormy ocean below. A passenger cried out in panic, "Somebody do something religious." The deacon got up and began taking a collection.

If our Lord had been asked the question "What does it mean to be religious?" he would probably have answered in one word—"service." This is what Jesus said he came to do. He said to his disciples, "The Son of man came not to be ministered unto, but to minister, and to give his life a ransom for many" (Matt. 20:28).

The Lord's service had very practical dimensions. He went looking for lost men who needed to be led to the Shepherd-God. He engaged in an active and demanding ministry of teaching and preaching. He cared about the sick and forgotten people and healed them. Finally, he rendered the ultimate service of offering himself as a sacrifice for others. The Lord said to his disciples, "Greater love hath no man than this, that a man lay down his life for his friends" (John 15:13). Jesus has that kind of love; and in demonstration of it, "While we were still sinners, Christ died for us" (Rom. 5:8, NIV).

The Christ who came to serve called and sent men to do the same. However, men can have the wrong idea about service. This was true of two of our Lord's followers—James and John. Salome, their mother, asked the Lord Jesus to allow her two sons to sit on his right and left hands in his kingdom. She was asking that her sons be given positions of honor. In response to the request, Jesus asked the two disciples if they could drink from his cup. The cup symbolized a life of service. William Barclay wrote, "It is quite wrong to think that for the Christian the cup must always mean the short, sharp, bitter, agonizing struggle of martyrdom; the cup may well be the long routine of the Christian life, with all of its daily sacrifices, its daily struggle, and its heartbreaks and its disappointments and its tears."[1]

Those two disciples did drink of the cup of service and found that the contents were a mixture of disappointment and dividends. Service is our business as we live toward a vision. In our service for the Master we also discover this strange mixture in the cup. A person must expect some disappointments in serv-

ice to the Lord Jesus Christ but he should also anticipate great
dividends.

The Frustration of Service

Serving can be an extremely frustrating experience. There
are some people who have the naive idea that when they are
doing what the Lord wants them to do, in the place where he
has put them, and in the manner he directs, all will be right
and success will be the result. But that is not the way it is.
Service has its wilderness places where one experiences difficulty
and disappointment.

One day a man came to Jesus saying, "Lord, I will follow
thee whithersoever thou goest" (Luke 9:57). That man was probably young, for there is enthusiasm and excitement in his statement. He doubtless saw the thrill and adventure associated with
the ministry of the Lord Jesus and wanted in on it. But in response to his burning enthusiasm, the Lord said, "Foxes have
holes, and birds of the air have nests; but the Son of man hath
not where to lay his head" (v.58). The Lord was saying that
there is more in service than just the thrill of adventure. There
is also difficulty and privation.

The Lord Christ spoke of these in personal terms. He experienced frustrations in service. No one would doubt that Jesus
Christ was in the center of God's will, doing what the Lord
sent him into the world to do. As a lad of twelve he said to
Mary and Joseph, "Wist ye not that I must be about my Father's
business?" (Luke 2:49). Later the Lord said to the people, "For
I came down from heaven, not to do mine own will, but the
will of him that sent Me" (John 6:38). Yet Christ knew frustrations in his service.

On at least two occasions Jesus visited his hometown of Nazareth. That was the place where he spent the major part of his

life. Nazareth was the place where he was best known. The Lord went home to do for the homefolks the things he was doing for people throughout Galilee. But the report of one of his visits to Nazareth ends with this sad statement of results; "And he could there do no mighty work save that he laid his hands upon a few sick folks, and healed them" (Mark 6:5). The reason for such a failure was the unbelief of the people of Nazareth. They saw the Lord Jesus as the carpenter and called him that. They knew him as the son of Mary and the brother of her other children. Because they saw him only as the carpenter and not as the Christ, they would not accept him. The Lord wanted to do so much for his own people, but he was frustrated in that desire.

The Lord Jesus also experienced frustration in service because of his disciples. He devoted so much of his time and energy to teaching and training them for service. But all James and John could think about was having seats of honor in Christ's kingdom. Peter, to whom the Lord looked to be a leader among the twelve, denied him three times at a time when Jesus needed his support. And Judas, to whom Christ reached out in love on so many occasions, sold him for thirty pieces of silver. Thus Jesus was frustrated at times because of the desires of those who were closest to him.

Service can be a frustrating experience for us. There is frustration when we fail to measure up to our sense of oughtness. Each one of us has a sense of what we ought to be and do. This applies to the activity of service, for we sense that we ought to do some things for Christ. Often we fail to measure up to that sense of oughtness; as a result, we know the frustration of failure.

I have the practice of making a list of the things I plan to do each week. At the beginning of the week I list all the things

I am obligated to do and then add other things I want to do or feel I ought to do. This list is kept handy as the week passes, and I check off each item as the work is done or an assignment is completed. At the end of the week I often experience the frustration of seeing that there were things I planned to do which were not done. Sometimes this frustration is the result of my sense of oughtness being too great. I planned to do more than was possible or necessary.

We can experience frustration in service when others do not want the ministry we desire to perform. Every Christian has his own "Nazareth experience" in which he wants to do something for someone who does not want anything done for him. You cannot help a person who does not want to be helped. Some Boy Scouts were reporting on the good deeds they had done. One Scout said, "Even though it took me thirty minutes, I helped a little old lady across the street." When he was asked why it took so long, he answered, "She didn't want to go across the street." But you cannot help those who refuse help. The refusal to be helped can cause us to be frustrated.

Then there is also the frustration of few results from our service. How many times we have known the experience of doing our best, yet there seemed to be no result. There are two facts, however, which will help us with this type of frustration. One is a truth my dad once stressed to me. I was blue because there seemed to be so few results in a time of service. My dad reminded me that my job was to be faithful in service and to leave the results to God. Also, it often takes time before results can be seen. A little boy went to the store and purchased some seeds. As soon as he got home he planted and watered them. Early the next morning he jumped up and ran outside, expecting to see a plant. We can have unrealistic expectations about results, and these can cause frustration.

The Fulfillment of Service

The Lord has promised that service will be fulfilling. What we do for the Lord God pays rich dividends. Paul wrote to the Galatians, "And let us not be weary in well-doing: for in due season we shall reap, if we faint not" (6:9). He also wrote to the Corinthians, "Therefore, my beloved brethren, be ye stedfast, unmoveable, always abounding in the work of the Lord, forasmuch as ye know that your labour is not in vain in the Lord" (1 Cor. 15:58).

The Lord Jesus experienced fulfillment in his ministry. One day he stopped at Jacob's well outside the city of Sychar. The disciples went to buy food and left Jesus resting by the well. A woman came at noon to draw water. The woman needed the water of life more than water from the well, and the Lord met that need in her life. When the disciples returned with the food they offered it to Jesus. The Lord said, "I have meat to eat that ye know not of" (John 4:32). The hungry, thirsty, and tired Christ had found satisfaction and fulfillment in helping the woman.

The Lord eventually went to his cross. He hung there for six hours, experiencing indescribable agony and pain plus the much greater torment of bearing our sins. But finally he said, "It is finished" (John 19:30). That was not a cry of resignation or defeat. It was the shout of triumph and victory. The Lord Jesus was declaring, "I have done what I came to do." There was the fulfillment of the finished work.

At the close of World War I, an artist was asked to paint a picture for the Royal Corps of Signalmen. The painting depicts a battlefield. Shells are exploding in the air and the ground is scarred by shell holes. There is barbed wire, discarded weapons, and the dead and dying everywhere. In the center of the picture there is a dead signal corpsman. In his lifeless hands he is holding together the two ends of a severed communication cable. The caption beneath the picture is only one word—"Through." The Lord Jesus knew the satisfaction of a finished job. On the cross the Lord said, "Through."

Christians today can experience fulfillment and satisfaction in serving the Lord. We can know the fulfillment of having done what the Lord put us here to do. Ralph Waldo Emerson said, "The greatest reward of a job well done is having done it." One of the greatest dividends in service is knowing you did what the Lord sent you to do.

To experience satisfaction in service we must find the job Christ put us here to do and then get busy at it. Serving in the consciousness that I am doing what the Lord wants me to do makes that service a means of fulfillment even in the midst of frustration. A pastor was called one night to go to a house in the poverty area of his city. A young mother was dying and the minister was needed. When he arrived at the house his knock at the door was answered by the six-year-old daughter of the woman. She looked up at the pastor and asked, "Are you from God?" He began to answer, "No, I'm from the First Baptist . . . ," and stopped. Then he said, "Yes, honey, I'm from God." Serving with the knowledge that we are from God gives our service a whole new dimension and makes it a fulfilling experience.

Our service can be fulfilling because of the contribution made to another person's life. What would any of us be apart from the contributions and investments made by others on our behalf? Think of parents, friends, pastors, teachers, and the one to whom God has led us in a relationship indescribable—where would we be without the investments these have made in us?

Having been the beneficiary of such self-giving on the part

of others, we are to do the same. Doing so brings a sense of satisfaction and fulfillment that cannot be equaled. One of the greatest dividends from service rendered is to have someone say to you, "My life is better because you touched it."

Several years ago I preached in a revival meeting in New York. The first service was on a Wednesday evening. Most of the people present were strangers to me, as I was to them. On Thursday evening when I arrived at the church, Mrs. Robert Fling, the pastor's wife, called my attention to a woman in the congregation. The woman had talked to Mrs. Fling that morning and told her that she had planned to commit suicide. Her husband was an alcoholic and her teenage daughters were giving her problems. In a state of despair, she made her plans to take her life, but decided to attend the revival service on Wednesday evening to give God one last chance to offer her hope. The woman told the pastor's wife that the Lord spoke to her through my message. She found the hope to go on living.

Some months later I was in New York on vacation and visited that church. The couple seated on the row ahead of me turned to welcome me as a visitor. It was that woman, and seated next to her was her husband. The sense of fulfillment I experienced then and now is indescribable.

We can find fulfillment and satisfaction in service by being aware that the Lord knows. The writer of the Hebrew epistle said, "Nothing in all creation is hidden from God's sight. Everything is uncovered and laid bare before the eyes of him to whom we must give account" (4:13, NIV). When the Lord Jesus addressed letters to the churches of Asia, he said to each, "I know thy works" (Rev. 2:2,9,13,19; 3:1,8,15).

There are so many who serve unseen in the out-of-the-way places of life. There is the retired man who delights in visiting the shut-ins in his church family. There is the woman who has given years of service in one department of small children in Sunday School. There is the pastor who belongs to "Ministers Anonymous" because he serves in small rural churches with no opportunity for recognition. There are the one-talent people whose services are faithfully performed in the dim shadows cast by the greatness of another. Who knows about these? No spotlight is ever focused on them; no words of praise are spoken in tribute to their service; no trophies and honors are given to them. And yet, the Lord Jesus knows.

The "well done" of the Master is spoken to the faithful servant on the basis of the Lord's firsthand knowledge of the person and what he did. Even though the service goes unnoticed and unapplauded by men, he knows; and in his own time he will speak his word of approbation.

Albert Schweitzer was a musician, writer, philosopher, surgeon, and missionary. He turned his back on fame and fortune and in 1913 went to Africa to serve uneducated natives. His first hospital was an abandoned hen house. His first operating table was an old cot. During a visit to America some years later, a newspaperman asked Dr. Schweitzer, "Have you found happiness in Africa?" He responded, "I have found a place of service, and this is enough for anyone." The great missionary knew fulfillment in service.

Conclusion

The 142 clergymen who were asked, "What does it mean to be religious?" gave a variety of answers. I believe our Lord would define being religious in terms of service. After all, that is what he did. He said that he did not come to be served, but to serve.

The serving Savior has called and sent us to serve. Some see this as a laborious obligation. They serve with an attitude which says, "This is something I must do, so let's get it over with."

The Bible teaches that service is a means of reaping great dividends. Even though a person does experience frustration, there is the joy of satisfaction and fulfillment which can only be experienced as one freely gives himself in service. This is indeed the dividend from the investment of life.

12
The Destiny of Life

Every journey should have a destination. Life is like a journey, and the destination for the Christian is heaven. The Lord Jesus told his disciples, "In my Father's house are many rooms; if it were not so, would I have told you that I go to prepare a place for you? And when I go and prepare a place for you, I will come again and will take you to myself, that where I am you may be also" (John 14:2-3, RSV).

What a place that must be! And how wonderful life must be in heaven. Rudyard Kipling expressed it this way in "L'Envoi":

> When Earth's last picture is painted,
> and the tubes are twisted and dried,
> When the oldest colors have faded,
> and the youngest critic has died,
> We shall rest, and, faith, we shall need it—
> lie down for an aeon or two,
> Till the Master of All Good Workmen
> shall put us to work anew.
>
> And those that were good shall be happy:
> they shall sit in a golden chair;
> They shall splash at a ten-league canvas
> with brushes of comet's hair;
> They shall find real saints to draw from—
> Magdalene, Peter, and Paul;

> They shall work for an age at a sitting,
> and never be tired at all!
>
> And only the Master shall praise us,
> and only the Master shall blame;
> And no one shall work for money,
> and no one shall work for fame;
> But each for the joy of working,
> and each in his separate star,
> Shall draw the Thing as he sees It
> for the God of Things as They Are! [1]

A little girl was walking one night with her father. She looked up and saw the stars sparkling like diamonds on black velvet. She said to her father, "If heaven with its stars is so beautiful on the bottom side, just think how wonderful it must be on the top side!"

To discover just how wonderful heaven is and what life will be like there, one must turn to the Bible. John the apostle, in exile on Patmos, was permitted to see that place not made with hands prepared by God for his own people. He wrote about what he saw and described heaven as a city. John said the angel took "me away in the spirit to a great and high mountain, and shewed me that great city, the holy Jerusalem, descending out of heaven from God" (Rev. 21:10). Then in Revelation 22:1-5 he described what life would be like in that glorious city of God. John wrote that heaven is a place of:

Life

In the city of God John saw a garden with a river and all kinds of trees. "And he shewed me a pure river of the water of life, clear as crystal, proceeding out of the throne of God and of the Lamb. In the midst of the street of it, and on either side of the river, was there the tree of life, which bare twelve manner of fruits, and yielded her fruit every month" (Rev. 22:1-2).

We do not need to guess or speculate about the meaning of the river and the tree. Both are described with the word life— the river of the water of life and the tree of life. These declare that heaven is a place of abundant and endless life which has its source in God.

When man first sinned, he was put out of the Garden of Eden. The reason for that expulsion was to keep him from eating of the tree of life (Gen. 3:22-23). The tree of life was in the midst of the Garden of Eden (Gen. 2:9), and sinful man had to be kept from eating its fruit lest he live forever in that place of indescribable beauty.

The ancient Jews thought of the dead as being in *Sheol*, the place of departed spirits. The Jews' first idea about *Sheol* was that it was a place of no memory or consciousness. Job, who lamented the fact of his birth and wished he had died then, said, "For then I should have lain down and been quiet;/I should have slept; then I should have been at rest" (Job 3:13, RSV). He later described *Sheol* as "the land of gloom and deep darkness,/the land of gloom and chaos, where light is as darkness" (10:21-22, RSV).

Heaven is not a place of a limbo-type existence. It is a place of life where those who belong to the Lord live on forever. I am impressed at how quickly we shift verb tenses when speaking of our deceased loved ones and friends. Instead of speaking of them in present-tense terms, we suddenly shift to the past tense: "John was such a fine person" or "Sue was so gracious." It is as if we are saying, "They no longer are alive." Not so, for heaven is a place of endless life with the Lord.

Not only is heaven a place of life; it is a place of:

Liberty

The Lord Jesus said, "If the Son therefore shall make you free, ye shall be free indeed" (John 8:36). Jesus Christ is the great liberator. When he went home to Nazareth and went into the synagogue on the sabbath, he chose a passage from Isaiah as his text. "The Spirit of the Lord is upon me, because he hath anointed me to preach the gospel to the poor; he hath sent me to heal the brokenhearted, to preach deliverance to the captives, and recovering of sight to the blind, to set at liberty them that are bruised, To preach the acceptable year of the Lord" (Luke 4:18-19). Jesus announced that he came to liberate enslaved men.

Even though we know freedom because of Christ on this side of death, it will not be until we get to heaven that we experience the full freedom and limitless liberty that will be ours. John wrote about two of life's realities from which those in heaven have liberty. The first of these is sickness. John said, "The leaves of the tree were for the healing of the nations" (Rev. 22:2).

Disease, pain, and physical suffering are realities of life today. Those of us whose service brings us into daily contact with people who are suffering from physical, mental, and emotional illnesses have learned that there are no simple answers to this human reality. Disease is no respecter of persons, entering the castles of the great with as much ease as it invades the houses of the poor. So many times sickness is a long and painful sentence which ends with the punctuation mark of death. But there is no disease or death in heaven. People in heaven have liberty from the sicknesses of this world.

Second, heaven is a place of liberty from sin. John wrote, "And there shall in no wise enter into it any thing that defileth, neither whosoever worketh abomination, or maketh a lie" (Rev. 21:27). He added, "And there shall be no more curse" (22:3).

Sin is a universal malady, and all of us have to deal with it daily. A burdened woman said to me, "I have sinned." She was speaking words true about all of us. The Lord Jesus can set men free from the penalty and power of sin, but in this world we must daily face the presence of sin. Adam's experience is every man's experience.

But in heaven we have liberty from sin. In 1833 a great event took place on the island of Jamaica. The British Parliament had voted to abolish slavery in all the colonies of the crown. Hardly a slave in Jamaica slept at all the night before the emancipation became effective. Instead, they dressed in their finest clothes and climbed the mountains to see the first gleams of a new day which would mean a new way of life. When the darkness began to give way to the light of day, the people erupted in unrestrained ecstasy. That day a new spiritual was born: "Free at last; free at last; thank God Almighty, free at last!" In heaven we shall finally put aside the enslaving chains of sin and sing the song of freedom.

Heaven is also a place of:

Likeness

John said that the people in heaven will have God's name on them. "And they shall see his face; and his name shall be in their foreheads" (Rev. 22:4). Having God's name on them speaks not only of God's ownership but of being like him. To wear God's name is to have a likeness to him.

Becoming like Jesus is the Christian's goal in life. The Lord God is at work in all things to make us like Jesus. Paul said that God is working to conform us to the image of his Son (Rom. 8:28-29).

Margaret Ann and I are the proud parents of two daughters and a son. Even though they may deserve sympathy, some people say that our older daughter and our son resemble me. That daughter recently presented us with a beautiful granddaughter. People say she looks just like her mother who, they say, looks like her father. I cannot help but be pleased with such comments. How much it must please the heavenly Father when we demonstrate likeness to him in the conduct of life.

Sadly, however, in spite of our desire to be like the Lord, we often are unchristlike in word and deed. It is said that there was a soldier in the army of Alexander the Great who had the same name as the famous leader. In one battle the soldier named Alexander behaved in a cowardly fashion. The report of this reached the Greek conqueror, who summoned the soldier. Alexander the Great said to the man, "Change your ways or change your name." As the Lord Christ sees our unchristlike behavior, he probably wants to say the same to us.

Even though being like Jesus is our goal in life, it will not be fully reached until we get to heaven. There we will have his name on our foreheads—we will be just like him. John wrote, "Beloved, now are we the sons of God, and it doth not yet appear what we shall be: but we know that, when he shall appear, we shall be like him; for we shall see him as he is" (1 John 3:2).

Heaven is also a place of:

Labor

Earlier in the Revelation John wrote that heaven is a place where men rest from their labors. "And I heard a voice from heaven saying unto me, Write, Blessed are the dead which die in the Lord from henceforth: Yea, saith the Spirit, that they may rest from their labours; and their works do follow them"

(14:13). This does not mean, however, that heaven is a place of idleness.

The word labor comes from the Greek word *kopon*. It is different from the usual word for work *(ergon)*. In the Greek, *kopon* speaks of painful and strenuous toil or work done at a great price. Service for Christ is often like that. Paul wrote of our labor for Christ and said it is not in vain (1 Cor. 15:58).

To say, however, that in heaven the Christian rests from his labors does not mean that he does nothing. There was an elderly woman who lived a hard life in which she was perpetually tired. One day she was asked what she was going to do when she got to heaven. She answered, "I'm going to sit in a rocking chair. After a thousand years or so, I may begin to rock."

A woman who had lived a difficult life had the following inscription put on her tombstone:

> Here lies a woman who was always tired
> For she lived in a world where too much was required.
> Weep not for me, friends, she said, for I'm going
> Where there'll neither be cooking nor washing nor sewing.
> I go where the loud hallelujahs are ringing,
> But I shall not take part in the singing.
> Then weep not for me, friends, if death do us sever,
> For I'm going to do nothing for ever and ever.[2]

Heaven is not a place of placid repose but a place of service. John mentioned two services we shall perform in heaven. First, we shall worship in heaven. The throne of God and of the Lamb will be in heaven, "and his servants will worship him" (Rev. 22:3*b*, TEV). Other passages in Revelation show the saints worshiping in heaven (4:9-11; 7:9-12).

There are many things we do on earth that we will never do in heaven. Jesus said there will be no marrying or giving in marriage in heaven (Mark 12:25). There will be no witnessing to the lost in heaven, for none will be there. We won't visit the sick, bury the dead, or build petty monuments to our glory in heaven. But we will worship. The one thing we do on earth that we will continue to do in heaven is worship the Lord. Everytime we go to worship in public or private we are preparing ourselves for the service of worship throughout eternity.

Second, John said that we will reign in heaven. "And they shall reign for ever and ever" (Rev. 22:5). Peter asked Jesus what he and the other disciples would receive since they had left all to follow him. The Lord answered, "Verily I say unto you, that ye which have followed me, in the regeneration when the Son of man shall sit in the throne of his glory, ye also shall sit upon twelve thrones, judging the twelve tribes of Israel" (Matt. 19:28). So heaven is a place where the redeemed shall share in the reign of the Redeemer.

Finally, John showed that heaven is a place of:

Light

The apostle wrote, "And there shall be no night there; and they need no candle, neither light of the sun; for the Lord God giveth them light" (Rev. 22:5). Christ, who is the light of the world (John 8:12), is also the light of heaven. "And the city had no need of the sun, neither the moon, to shine in it: for the glory of God did lighten it, and the Lamb is the light thereof" (Rev. 21:23).

Light is synonymous with knowledge and understanding, while darkness represents ignorance. These are the meanings given to light and darkness in the Bible. The psalmist wrote: "They have neither knowledge nor understanding,/they walk about in darkness" (82:5, RSV); and "The unfolding of thy words gives light;/it imparts understanding to the simple" (119:130, RSV). The cartoonist's usual way of picturing an idea or sudden understanding is to draw a light bulb.

John's statement about heaven's being a place of light means that in heaven we will see things and understand events that are a mystery and puzzle to us now. Paul said, "For now we see through a glass, darkly; but then face to face: now I know in part; but then shall I know even as also I am known" (1 Cor. 13:12).

So many times question marks the size of skyscrapers loom in our minds. Try as we may, we cannot understand so many things that happen. We are forced to finally admit that we simply do not know. One Sunday my son and I were riding home together from church. He asked me a question, wanting me to explain something to him. I did not know the answer and frankly admitted my ignorance. He looked at me and exclaimed, "You don't know! You're a preacher; you're supposed to know everything!" I quickly corrected that false idea about preachers and others as well.

There are so many things we do not know and events we are incapable of explaining. However, in heaven that will be changed. Then we shall see and understand. And we shall discover that God had his purpose and plan even though it was unseen and unknown by us.

My mother does needlepoint as a hobby. I have picked up some of her work and looked at it. One side, the one not to be seen when the work is finished, is a mass of loose threads and meaningless lines. But in turning the needlepoint over I would discover a beautiful design. We look at life from the bottom side, but in heaven we will see and know all of God's plan.

Conclusion

Heaven is like a great city—a city the Lord God has built for his people. In that city the redeemed have life, liberty, labor, likeness, and light. The wonder of that place is greater than we can imagine. Paul wrote, "Eye hath not seen, nor ear heard, neither have entered into the heart of man, the things which God hath prepared for them that love him" (1 Cor. 2:9).

This great city is our destiny in Christ. A man had tuberculosis and moved to the country to recover. One day a friend visited him and the man said to his visitor, "Tomorrow I'm going to return to the city." Time passed and the friend did not see the man or hear of his return to the city. He went back to the country estate and found the man near death. He said, "I thought you said you were going to return to the city." The dying man answered, "I am going to a city, but it will be a city where the living never die, and where no sickness and sorrow can come."

Following the man's death his friend remembered his words and wrote:

> I am going to a city where the living never die,
> Where no sickness and no sorrow can molest;
> From the body to release me, Christ is speeding from on high;
> He will greet me and escort me to my rest.[3]

Notes

Chapter 2

1. C. Roy Angell, *Baskets of Silver* (Nashville: Broadman Press, 1955), pp. 58-59.
2. William Ernest Henley, "Invictus," in James Dalton Morrison, ed., *Masterpieces of Religious Verse* (Nashville: Broadman Press, 1977).
3. John Ehrlichman, quoted by Nick Thimmesch in *New York Magazine*.
4. Dietrich Bonhoeffer, *The Cost of Discipleship* (New York: The Macmillan Company, 1963), p. 97.
5. Ibid., p. 99.

Chapter 3

1. John Homer Miller, *Tarbell's Teacher's Guide*, 1978-1979, pp. 159-160.

Chapter 4

1. Erich Fromm, *Man for Himself* (New York: Holt, Rinehart, and Winston), p. 91.

Chapter 5

1. Ralph L. Woods, *Wellsprings of Wisdom* (Norwalk, Conn.: The C. R. Gibson Company, 1969), pp. 67-68.
2. Erich Fromm, *The Art of Loving* (New York: Harper & Row, 1956), p. 51.
3. Cecil Osborne, *The Art of Learning to Love Yourself* (Grand Rapids: Zondervan Publishing House, 1976), p. 11.
4. Ibid., p. 105.

CHAPTER 6

1. *Speaker's Illustrations for Special Days,* p. 128.

CHAPTER 8

1. Charles L. Allen, *Roads to Radiant Living* (Old Tappan, New Jersey: Fleming H. Revell Company, 1973), pp. 81-82.
2. Roger Crook, *How to Be Nervous and Enjoy It* (Nashville: Broadman Press, 1975).

CHAPTER 9

1. As stated in *Redbook,* January 1979, pp. 83, 138-141.
2. David Mace, in an address entitled "Love, Anger, and Intimacy" presented to the Christian Life Commission, "Help for Families," Orlando, Florida, March 28, 1979.
3. Derrick Sherwin Bailey, *The Mystery of Love and Marriage* (New York: Harper & Row, 1952), p. 44.

CHAPTER 10

1. Louis H. Evans, *Make Your Faith Work* (Westwood, New Jersey: Fleming H. Revell Company, 1957), p. 69.
2. J. B. Phillips, *Letters to Young Churches* (New York: The Macmillan Company, 1952), p. 195.
3. Curtis Vaughan, *James, a Study Guide* (Grand Rapids: Zondervan Publishing House, 1969), p. 70.
4. L. Nelson Bell, *Christianity Today,* 31 July 1961, p. 24.
5. Alexander Pope, "The Temple of Flame," in H. L. Mencken, ed., *A New Dictionary of Quotations on Historical Principles from Ancient and Modern Sources* (New York: Alfred A. Knopf, 1962), p. 479.
6. Earl Kelly, *James: a Primer for Christian Living* (Nutley, New Jersey: The Craig Press, 1969), p. 65.
7. Vaughan, p. 73.

CHAPTER 11

1. William Barclay, *The Gospel of Matthew,* vol. 2, The Daily Study Bible (Philadelphia: The Westminster Press), p. 254.

CHAPTER 12

1. Rudyard Kipling, "L'Envoi," in James Dalton Morrison, ed., *Masterpieces of Religious Verse* (Nashville: Broadman Press, 1977), p. 602.

2. Donald W. Richardson, *The Revelation of Jesus Christ* (Richmond: John Knox Press, 1964), p. 136.

3. Ibid., p. 138.